WEISS RESEARCH, INC.
P. O. Box 2923
W. Palm Beach, FL 33402

THE GREAT MONEY PANIC

THE GREAT MONEY PANIC

Martin D. Weiss

ARLINGTON HOUSE PUBLISHERS
Westport, Connecticut

Distributed by:
MARTIN D. WEISS RESEARCH, INC.
2000 Palm Beach Lakes Blvd.
West Palm Beach, FL 33409

For my wife, Elisabeth

Library of Congress Cataloging in Publication Data

Weiss, Martin D.
The great money panic.

Edition for 1975 published under title:
The money panic.
Includes index.
1. Inflation (Finance)—United States. 2. United
States—Economic conditions—1971-   3. Investments.
I. Title.
HG540.W46   1981   332.4'1'0973   80-29444
ISBN 0-87000-502-2

Design by Sam Gantt

Illustrations by Sam Rawls (SCRAWLS)

MANUFACTURED IN THE UNITED STATES OF AMERICA

9 8 7 6 5 4 3

Contents

BOOK III.   THE PANIC

BOOK IV.   THE RECOVERY

Introduction

I AM WRITING this book to warn you that the American economy is on the brink of the Great Money Panic.

The Great Money Panic is not the same recession repeating itself every few years until the far reaches of the next century. Nor is it the Great Depression returning to haunt us from the depths of the 1930s. The Great Money Panic is entirely different from anything we have ever experienced: a boomerang reaction to decades of accelerated expansion; an outpouring of stockpiled goods; a sudden contraction in consumption, production, and distribution; an historic shift in values and behavior patterns; and, most important, an explosive demand for cash.

Does the Government have the will or the power to prevent it? I believe the answer to that is *no!* An easy-money policy revives the fear of inflation and triggers a bond-market collapse. A tight-money policy chokes cash-starved corporations and creates an instant credit crunch. And a hands-off policy forfeits the fate of the economy to the most powerful force of all—a gargantuan *one trillion dollars* in short-term debts coming due within the next twelve months. It threatens to set into motion a unique vicious circle wherein declining business and cash shortages feed on each other, generating an uncontrollable rise in interest rates.

Those who believe our Government will resolve this crisis by taking the easy way out are wrong. They believe that the politicians will pounce on the interest-rate kangaroo with a wild expansionary thrust; let the banks make loans without normal reserves; funnel cash directly into bankrupt companies; and, above all, *print* money.

Although some initial steps may be taken in that direction, our leaders will soon be forced to retreat to a more neutral stance. Here's why: In February 1980 an event occurred in New York City—and in other financial capitals of the world—that most have yet to comprehend fully: *Bond markets suffered the greatest collapse in history.* First, the buyers disappeared. Then most dealers abandoned the marketplace. Finally the entire market came to a near closedown, making it next to impossible for the Government to borrow the funds it needed to run this country. Our leaders were faced with only two choices: risk an eventual default— implying the end of the Government itself—or else DEFLATE. They chose, and probably will continue to choose, the latter.

Millions of individuals and thousands of institutions own $4.4 trillion in U.S. Government bonds, corporate bonds, municipal bonds, mortgages and loans—*three and a half times as much as all common and preferred stocks in America.* These investors and creditors have already suffered huge losses in their portfolios due, in part, to inflation. If they become convinced that there will soon be a recovery and more inflation, they will *sell* their holdings and cause another bond-market collapse. The Government will be forced to deflate again.

Is there still hope for this country? The answer to that question is *yes!*

Allowing for exceptional areas, I do not go along with the belief that there will be widespread social chaos and revolution. The Great Money Panic, as I see it, is an intense but beneficial housecleaning process that will help correct imbalances and distortions deeply embedded in the structure of society. Despite the temporary upheaval and unhappiness, it can also become an opportunity for us to stop, reorganize, cooperate, and adjust our productive system to the real needs of the future.

The purpose of this book is to contribute, if in only a small way, to this opportunity. By predicting a crisis, I am not yelling "fire" in a crowded cinema. I am uncovering very real financial hazards lurking behind the still strong-looking facade of business and banking.

Book One delves into the weaknesses of General Motors, AT&T, and Sears, Roebuck; electric utilities, commercial banks, and savings and loan institutions. I demonstrate that virtually every economic institution of the nation is inflexible, illiquid, and ill-prepared for the crisis ahead. In Book Two I suggest what I believe you can do about the Great Money Panic—not only to survive, but to come out ahead in the months and years that follow.

In Book Three I explore how events will unfold in the future. Finally, in Book Four, I develop a scenario for the recovery. Whether there will be a recovery is not a question of economic forecast or philosophical debate. It is a matter of choice. Our nation is not a war-ravaged Germany of the 1920s or a capital-starved developing country. We have, and will continue to have for many years to come, a great capacity to produce, to adapt, and to compete. We have the technology, the skill, and, above all, the creativity needed to confront this and other crises down the road.

Although I often use the past tense for many events taking place today, as well as events that I believe will take place in the future, I want to make clear that I have no crystal ball. As time goes by and you compare the events taking place with those predicted in this book, you will inevitably find some that match well, but some that do not. No one can predict the future with precision. You will also discover, however, that my forecast of a major financial crisis is grounded on extensive analysis, giving you the knowledge you will need to protect yourself and your family from the impending disaster.

New York, N.Y.
August 5, 1980

BOOK

I

The
Superboom

"CREEPING INFLATION? SURE—WHY NOT?
LET'S TRY SOME OF THAT CREEPING INFLATION."

1

Project Explosion

FOUR MEN SIT QUIETLY in the executive conference room of the ABC Retailers of America awaiting the arrival of the chairman. A slightly bald, middle-aged executive walks into the room, plops his briefcase on the table, and pulls out a yellow pad. There is an extra touch of arrogance in his voice as he begins to speak.

"Our expansion strategies were all right for the early sixties, but this is a new era. We need a new strategy, a new plan, a new philosophy."

It is the winter of 1976, and business volume is picking up rapidly from the recession. Such strategy meetings are being held in one corporation after another throughout the country to plan for what will prove to be one of the longest periods of uninterrupted expansion in modern U.S. history—the superboom of the late seventies. Some firms are hesitant because of the close call with financial insolvency in 1975. But ABC is one of the first to switch back into the gung-ho philosophy that predominated before the crunch—and soon most other companies follow the lead.

"But, Mr. Chairman," queries an assistant, "the last plan we called 'project acceleration.' What shall we call the plan this time?"

"Project Explosion! Of course."

"Ah, yes. Of course."

The financial vice-president is somewhat perplexed. "But haven't we already borrowed heavily from the banks? Aren't we already expanding as fast as physically possible? What *more* can we do?"

"The trouble with us," answers the chairman, "is that we imbue liquid assets with a positive value, and liabilities with a negative value. Most of us were brought up with the idea that savings are good and debt is bad. But now we must struggle to purge ourselves of the prejudices and fears of bygone generations. It is time to declare war on cash! I have two strategies. First, the 'octopus strategy'—eight new ways of squeezing fresh cash out of the nation's money supply.

"Number one," he continues, counting on his fingers, "we tap the banks, playing one against the other if necessary. Either the banks say 'yes' or they lose our business.

"Number two: We float larger bond issues to the public—and when I say float, I really mean *drown*. Drown them in our bonds.

"Number three: We push our commercial paper, we give 'em the best rate we can. Show them we mean business!"

(Commercial paper represents IOUs sold by a corporation in the open market in order to raise money from other corporations or from individual investors.)

"What rate?" interrupts the financial vice-president again.

"Nine percent, maybe more!"

"What? You're nuts," he half whispers impulsively. "Excuse my ignorance, but can we really afford it?"

"Of course! With the kind of return we're getting on our investment now, we can afford practically anything within reason. So what if the funds cost more? Inflation will soon be running nearly at that rate anyhow. The important thing is, the money is *there*. It's there for the taking.

"Number four: Don't hesitate to borrow Eurodollars from overseas. After all, originally it's *our* dollars, the money we've invested in our subsidiaries, that's floating around in the Eurodollar market out there; so what harm could there be in getting the banks to borrow some for us?"

"You don't need the local banker. Just have our London subsidiary phone the London banker directly," says one of the vice-presidents, echoing the chairman's enthusiasm.

"Right! Good idea! Number Five: More common stock. Let 'em have it. This stock market has got enough money floating around to finance anything we damn please, and the stock prices will still make new highs.

"Number six: Preferred stock.

"Number seven: Get our European subsidiaries to float their own bonds denominated in foreign currencies—the Eurobond market. Let's tap that Eurobond market."

There's a brief silence. The five men imagine cash coming in from all sides, new shopping centers springing up all over the country.

"Is that everything?" asks the financial vice-president.

"That's it! That's the octopus strategy."

"But what about the eighth one?" retorts his assistant.

"Oh, of course, the most important one." He lowers his voice as if speaking in confidence. "Go find yourselves a few sweet little companies that have been sitting on their butts with a hoard of cash and—*take them over!*"

The men in the conference room are impressed, and also astounded. They need time to digest it all. They begin to slam shut their attaché cases and prepare to leave.

"Wait a minute," shouts the chairman. "Where do you think you're going? I haven't told you yet about the second strategy—'hot potato.' While we're getting all that cash from the banks, the bond markets, the commercial paper, the stock market, the Eurodollar and the Eurobond markets, while we're swinging with the octopus, we simultaneously implement the 'hot potato.'"

"What's that?"

"A nationwide network of consumer finance companies that dish out cash to the consumer. Have you seen *this?*" The chairman tosses onto the conference table a plastic-covered report entitled "Recent Changes in Mass Consumer Psychology." Hastily drawn below the title is a stretched dollar bill with an oversized Idaho potato in the place of the familiar likeness of George Washington. "This is the 'hot potato study,' just completed by our consumer research group. Here's what it says: 'After the close encounter with double-digit inflation in 1974, something clicked in the psyche of the American consumer. As a result, we expect he is going to do more than just spend money. Next year he is going to double up on his mortgage. He's going to borrow from every possible source. He's going to run to the finance companies, the credit unions, and his neighborhood savings and loan. And then, you know what he's going to do? He's going to bend over backward to get rid of that cash as fast as he possibly can—to load up with durable goods.'"

"I see, you mean the old buy-now-pay-later routine."

"Nope. I mean the *new* borrow-now-or-else-pay-*more*-later routine. This is a wild consumer roller coaster we're riding. If we hang on firm, if we ride this new phase of the inflationary spiral, we'll prosper. If we try to buck it, we'll be left behind, squeezed out by the competition and gobbled up by some other cash-hungry giant."

The financial vice-president tries to get up his courage to protest. He isn't by any means a financial conservative, and, in fact, the old "project acceleration" was his own brainchild. But this new project explosion? Hot potato? Octopus? The chairman is going too far. "But isn't this all too risky and potentially dangerous?" he suggests in a low voice.

"Danger? *What* danger?"

"I mean our *cash liquidity,* our *quick liquidity ratio.* The thin ice of cash. We've got $499 million in debts coming due within the next twelve months. But we've got only $25 million or so in bank deposits, Government securities, and other holdings. Which means that for every dollar in short-term debts we've got only about 5 cents in cash and equivalent; our quick liquidity ratio is down to 5 percent! Suppose there's a strike. Suppose there's something unexpected. We still haven't licked the business cycle completely."

"That's where you're wrong. First of all, this economy is being fine-tuned as never before; the business cycle is just a trickle at our feet. So what if there's a strike? Have you forgotten we've got revolving standby credit arrangements with the banks? So we run out of liquid funds for a couple of days. So what? We just borrow more."

"But suppose there's a recession."

"Whaddayamean 'suppose.' We *already had* the recession. But *now* look! It's all over! The Government saved the day; and it will do precisely the same thing next time around. Besides, if there's a recession coming, we'll know ahead of time. That's what our computer surveys of consumer buying plans are for. Don't you see? This is no longer the hit-or-miss marketing system of the old days. Now we're in control. Now we know what the consumer is going to do well in advance, even before he *himself* knows. When you've got that kind of information, you don't need as much cash lying around as you used to."

The Lowest Liquidity of The Century

To a certain degree the chairman of ABC Retailers Corporation was correct. "Proper" or "normal" liquidity was no longer in the same range as it used to be and, so corporations could make do with less cash than in the old days. Yet there were two problems associated with this rationale.

First, it was usually assumed that the economic system was depression-proof; that prosperity was eternal and everlasting; that any business decline would be gradual and slow, never sudden and swift; and that even if there were to be a recession, there would always be time to retreat. It would be neither deep nor steep.

Second, after the corporations went through all the motions of setting up new, lower limits for their cash positions, they simply went ahead and ignored them anyhow, letting their bank balances drop still further and current debts pile up even more. In the end, expansionist strategies of the kind used at ABC Retailers produced record sales and earnings, but these strategies also dragged them closer to the brink of financial insolvency:

Graph 1 shows the changes from 1910 through 1980 in the average quick liquidity (cash on hand to meet short-term debts) of a sample of ten large American corporations—AT&T, Anaconda, Du Pont, General Electric, General Motors, Goodyear Tire, International Harvester, Sears, Roebuck, U.S. Steel, and Westinghouse

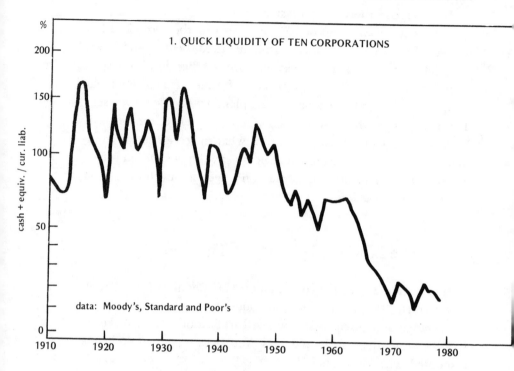

1. QUICK LIQUIDITY OF TEN CORPORATIONS

data: Moody's, Standard and Poor's

Electric. (Anaconda was dropped from the sample after 1975.) In the first half of the twentieth century they repeatedly built up large cash reserves in bad times and allowed them to dwindle in good times, always careful to maintain a minimum of cash for contingencies. Quick liquidity fluctuated sharply, but never below 70 percent. In the second half of the century these corporations drained their cash steadily and took on unprecedented amounts of short-term debt; except for a brief pause during the Eisenhower years, liquidity declined from a high of 127 percent in 1946 to a twentieth-century low of 16 percent at the end of 1979. This meant that for every dollar of debt coming due within one year they had only *sixteen cents* in cash!

High liquidity implied good flexibility, a reserve of power and resources that could easily and quickly be transferred into something else. Low liquidity implied *in*flexibility—excessive commitments to maintain factories and equipment or to pay off debts.

In more concrete terms, high liquidity came with the ownership of cash and securities equivalent to cash, such as U.S. Government bonds, Treasury notes, or Treasury bills. Low liquidity came with the ownership of fixed assets that were difficult to get rid of—plant and equipment, real estate—and, above all, with *debts*.

Machinery and real estate were commitments to the past. Debts were commitments to the future. Cash, on the other hand, was immediately available for adjusting to the changing conditions in *the present*.

Normally, larger corporations were considered less vulnerable to financial trouble than smaller ones. Whenever there was a cash crisis, they could take advantage of their higher credit ratings and, with the sheer weight of their economic power, gain access to new sources of credit to ease their financial woes. But by the end of the

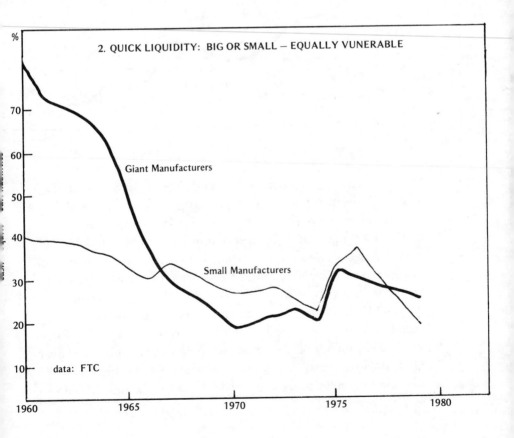

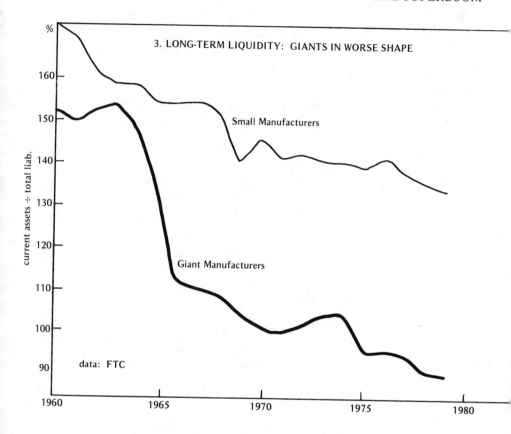

big boom, after having borrowed themselves out of one crisis after another, it was often these larger corporations that ironically became the more vulnerable to a major panic. Graph 2 illustrates that in 1960 manufacturing corporations with a billion dollars or more in assets were far more liquid than the smaller manufacturers. But with the unrestrained expansion of the superboom the giants drained their cash much faster than the small corporations. By 1979 both were in equally bad shape. If we look at *all* debts, including both short- and long-term, the contrast is even greater. Whereas in 1963 both the small and giant manufacturers had over $1.50 in current assets for every dollar of debts, in the year 1979 the small manufacturers still had $1.24, but the giants were down to 79 cents (graph 3).

Big debts meant big interest costs. When bracing oneself for a crisis, labor costs could be slashed with layoffs, and construction costs might be eliminated through cuts in expansion programs. But interest costs loomed as a Loch Ness monster, which, when business sank, could often drag any corporation, no matter how well prepared for a recession, into red ink.

For such large corporations as Ford and AT&T interest payments had grown so large that, by 1980, they were paying out to their creditors—in the form of interest—more than they had distributed to their stockholders in the form of dividends. Some critics from within and without did warn of the dangers of high, fixed interest costs, but they were snowed under by constant reassurances from the Federal Government that interest rates would be anchored down to reasonable levels. All the Presidents between 1960 and 1980—Kennedy, Johnson, Nixon, Ford, and Carter—promised at one time or another to hold interest rates down. As a result, the corporations borrowed without inhibition and entered a period of highly accelerated business activity, record-breaking sales revenues, and unrestrained expansion on all fronts.

Later, during the Great Money Panic, most U.S. corporations would come face to face with their day of reckoning. Which ones would survive? Which ones would fail?

As a general rule of thumb, if, by the end of the boom, a company showed an index close to 100 percent (a dollar in cash and equivalent for every dollar in current debt), if it made no radical changes in financial strategy, and if it suffered no major calamity, it would be more or less assured of financial survival.

On the other hand, if it had under thirty cents for every dollar of current debt, and if daily cash inflows suddenly fell sharply, or if, for some reason, it had to pay up some of the current debts right away, it was then forced to sell off inventories, receivables, and plants. Finally, in the event that it couldn't find a buyer or raise cash elsewhere, it could be wiped out, finished, bankrupt.

Table 1 shows that, as of year-end 1979, eleven major industrial companies had quick liquidity ratios *lower than 5 percent;* and seventeen, between 5 and 10 percent. In addition, there were sixteen major companies with between 10 and 30 percent.

TABLE 1
The Least Liquid Industrial Giants of America

Cash and equivalent as a percent of short-term debts			
Company	1979	1974	1970
Charter Co.	19.1	13.5	32.0
Gulf & Western Industries	19.0	31.3	18.2
Continental Group	18.9	15.3	16.8
Honeywell	18.7	8.7	21.2
Atlantic Richfield	17.9	44.2	35.4
Borden	17.3	23.1	46.7
McDonnell Douglas	17.1	0.5	7.0
Coca-Cola	16.8	95.6	68.3
Mobil Oil	16.8	19.2	49.1
National Steel	16.7	56.3	13.3
CBS	15.9	64.5	27.0
General Motors	15.3	14.2	47.1
FMC	15.0	1.5	9.4
Signal Companies	14.8	55.3	25.0
W. R. Grace	14.5	20.4	18.6
Republic Steel	14.5	53.1	16.1
Ford Motor Company	14.1	9.4	26.8
Owens Illinois	13.9	15.0	15.5
Sperry Rand	13.8	3.0	18.1
Chrysler	13.4	2.7	11.3
Occidental Petroleum	13.3	29.4	51.6
CPC International	13.2	6.7	73.0
Consolidated Foods	11.3	3.7	14.8
Marathon Oil	11.2	18.9	17.9
R. J. Reynolds	11.1	5.8	16.7
United Brands	11.0	41.8	56.4
Caterpillar Tractor	10.6	9.9	6.8
RCA	9.6	27.3	25.1
Dow Chemical	9.6	26.9	15.0
Allied Chemical	9.4	22.1	14.9
Armco Steel	9.0	35.2	10.0
Firestone Tire & Rubber	8.4	9.9	20.8
Amerada Hess	8.2	20.6	33.7
LTV	8.0	40.3	16.5
TRW	7.8	9.8	23.3
Champion International	7.2	15.3	13.9
Greyhound	7.2	20.5	76.3
United Tech	6.7	21.4	10.9
Lockheed Aircraft	6.4	15.7	15.7
American Brands	6.4	2.8	8.5
General Dynamics	5.6	3.3	1.1
Goodyear Tire & Rubber	5.4	7.4	8.3
Inland Steel	5.2	19.9	9.7
I.C. Industries	5.0	9.3	35.3
Philip Morris	4.9	7.4	13.6
Bendix	4.7	8.0	17.0
Eaton	4.5	15.6	11.3
Textron	4.2	8.8	28.4
American Can	4.1	15.7	13.2
International Harvester	3.6	4.3	16.3
IT&T	3.4	7.0	13.9
Esmark	3.3	7.7	20.2
Georgia Pacific	3.3	23.6	23.4
Tenneco	3.2	8.1	32.5
Deere	1.3	8.0	5.7

Data: Annual reports, Standard & Poor's (includes captive finance subsidiaries).

The first group (below 5 percent) included American Can, Bendix, Deere, Esmark, General Telephone & Electronics, Georgia Pacific, International Harvester, IT&T, Philip Morris, Tenneco, and Textron.

The second group (between 5 and 10 percent), also in the danger zone, included Allied Chemical, Amerada Hess, American Brands, Armco Steel, Champion International, Dow Chemical, Firestone Tire & Rubber, General Dynamics, Goodyear Tire & Rubber, Greyhound, I.C. Industries, Inland Steel, Lockheed Aircraft, LTV, RCA, TRW, and United Technologies.

The third group (between 10 and 30 percent) included such well-known blue-chip companies as Du Pont, Exxon, Ford, General Electric, General Motors, Mobil Oil, U.S. Steel, and many others not listed in this table. There were also some exceptional business managements that refused to go along with the crowd. They took the stand that the boom had reached its limits and that, even if a bit more growth could be squeezed out of the economy through artificial means, *they* didn't want to be a part of it. For example, the board of directors of Ashland Oil Corporation made the decision to sell off some oil properties to raise cash, drawing stinging criticism from Wall Street analysts that "they were missing the boat." The decision may have been somewhat premature. But months later, when the spot price for crude oil began to plummet and cash liquidity became a key to financial survival, it was a new ball game. Other companies that built up good cash were American Home Products (102 percent), Standard Oil of Ohio (89 percent), Eastman Kodak (88 percent), and Boeing (84 percent). Some might soon lose much of this cash unless they knuckled down faster to the onrushing economic crisis. Others might be able to hold their own. In either event, they remained the exception and not the rule.

As illustrated in the bar graphs, the liquidity problems pervaded every major industry group: the auto manufacturers, airlines, electric utilities, railroads, and steel producers. All showed decisively lower liquidity than in 1946. And, with the exception of the electric equipment manufacturers, every group let its cash positions deteriorate between 1976 and 1979. Later, even the big oil companies began to lose liquidity.

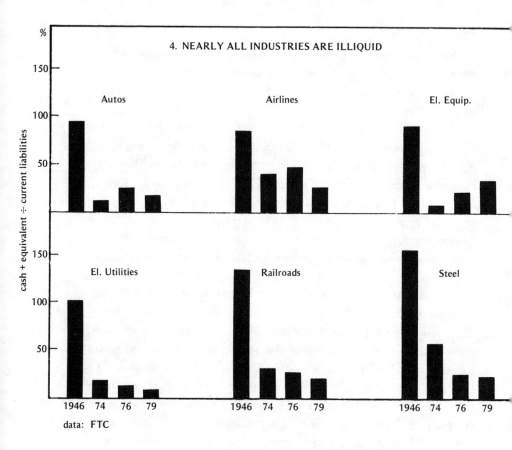

4. NEARLY ALL INDUSTRIES ARE ILLIQUID

cash + equivalent ÷ current liabilities

Autos • Airlines • El. Equip. • El. Utilities • Railroads • Steel

1946 74 76 79

data: FTC

Sweeping It Under The Rug

Liquidity crises flared up with the regularity of a nuclear clock—every four years: 1966, 1970, 1974. In 1966 interest rates soared, and the banks were swamped by cash-hungry corporate giants and forced to sell off bonds in order to raise money. In 1970 many corporations suddenly found that they didn't have enough cash on hand to pay off commercial paper—short-term IOUs sold to institutions and the public at large. The commercial paper crisis brought Penn Central to the ground and Chrysler Corporation to its knees. In 1974 Chrysler again began to encounter difficulties in rolling over commercial paper as nearly $3/4 billion were redeemed by mid-December; a large offering of long-term notes was canceled; and finally Moody's refused to give them a credit rating. Moreover, the liquidity crisis threatened to spread to other major corporations. Du Pont, for example, which had overcommitted itself to new expansion projects, saw its liquidity fall from 47 percent at the end of 1973 to 14 percent by mid-1974, and was forced to borrow heavily in the bond market to replenish its cash. In roughly the same period Xerox also suffered a sharp decline in short-term liquidity—from 48 percent to 4 percent—and was forced to cancel plans for a new headquarters complex in Stamford, Connecticut.

In 1966, 1970, and 1974 the Government stepped in and helped pump more credit into the system. Each time it was said that the crisis was over, that the dangers had passed, and that the problems were solved. In reality, each liquidity crisis was followed by larger and larger waves of short-term borrowing, producing lower and lower liquidity ratios for the corporations. Nothing was solved. The impending corporate disaster was merely postponed, and in the interim the underlying financial problems worsened.

In May and June of 1980 large corporations sought to sweep the short-term debts under the rug once again by borrowing from Peter to pay Paul. During a record-breaking bond-market rally they raised an estimated $12½ billion through the issuance of medium-term notes and long-term bonds, of which I estimate the giant manufacturing firms got only $4 billion. Yet in the preceding twelve months these manufacturers had borrowed $18 billion of short-term money from banks and the commercial paper market. Thus the new long-term money borrowed from "Peter" in the spring of 1980 was a drop in the bucket in comparison with the massive amounts borrowed from Paul during the 1979 boom. By midyear 1980 these giants (excluding the oil companies) still had total short-term debts of an estimated $161 billion versus cash and equivalent of only $21 billion—*a net cash deficit of approximately $140 billion.*

If this was true while corporate earnings were still not too far from their boomtime peaks, what would happen when earnings declined still further while short-term debts continued to come due? *A dominolike bankruptcy crisis* was imminent.

As you shall see in the chapters to come, liquidity was only one of the many problems confronting the corporate world.

2

When GM Thought It Could Predict the Future

BACK IN 1929 General Motors was well prepared for the big bust in the automobile market. During the Great Money Panic it was not.

William C. Durant incorporated General Motors in 1908 as an offshoot of the reorganized Buick Motor Company. He increased the variety of styles and engineering possibilities, integrating the manufacture of parts with the assembly itself. Whereas Maxwell, Nash, Hudson, and others fell into oblivion, General Motors thrived.

The first big expansion program was started in 1918 with a relatively heavy investment of over $280 million in plant, equipment, and subsidiary companies. Total sales volume doubled from $270 million to $567 million. GM was going great guns. But that was only on the surface. Despite the big successes, neither the executive committee nor the finance committee had the information they needed or the necessary control over the divisions. The divisions continued to spend lavishly, and their requests for additional funds were always over the budget. By the end of 1919 cash reserves were being quickly exhausted, and it was recommended that cash surpluses be provided to meet increased capital requirements should a serious recession in business occur, or should plants be suddenly shut down because of strikes extending over a period of several months. But no such action was ever taken.

The business slump of 1920 came as a complete surprise. Total inventories rose from $137 million in January 1920 to $209 million in October of that year, exceeding by $59 million the limits that were set by management in May. Because of this overexpansion GM's quick liquidity fell to 41 percent. Its former chairman, Alfred P. Sloan, Jr., writes in *My Years with General Motors*: "When the bottom fell out of the automobile market that fall, General Motors was caught red-handed, and operations were soon a shambles." Managers had insufficient cash available to pay invoices and payrolls; car producing divisions were either shut down entirely or operating at reduced rates; and Durant, who had tried to support the price of GM stock single-handed, was wiped out and forced by circumstances to resign.

Fortunately for GM, the Du Ponts stepped in. With the backing of Wall Street banking interests, they soon took control of all operations and moved quickly to rebuild liquidity. By December 1924 $1.78 of cash was available to cover every dollar of short-term debt. Between 1926 and 1929 investment in plant and equipment was again stepped up to meet a new boom in the automobile market. But the expansion was cautious. While the banks, the brokers, and the speculators plunged ahead into the roaring twenties, General Motors and other corporations held back. In other words, by 1929, since the fear of crisis was still fresh in mind, financial control—conspicuously absent before 1920—was now the prime concern. When the big crash finally hit, General Motors was not caught out on a limb, but was well prepared and flexible enough to withstand the storm. Alfred Sloan summed it up succinctly in these words:

"As a result of the speed with which we acted when the sales began to fall, we were able to reduce inventories in line with the sales decline and to control costs so that operations remained profitable."

Though sales declined 71 percent, inventories were reduced only 60 percent. Net income fell $248 million, but GM managed to earn $165,000 in 1932 while paying out $63 million in dividends. *At the low point of the crash GM actually made a profit.* Production slowed, but did not shut down. Profits dropped, but remained in the black. Markets were drowned in a wave of selling, but the firm kept its head above water. Most important, management at General Motors moved swiftly to improve liquidity. By the time the bottom of the crash was reached, it had built up more cash reserves than ever before—$1.84 of cash and equivalent per dollar of current debt.

Soon after business reached rock bottom General Motors was ready to reapply this reserve of cash power, boost sales, and help pull the United States out of the more extreme depths of the depression. In 1980, however, the picture was quite different.

The Age of Certainty

The history of GM can be divided into two eras: The first between 1908 and 1941, when there were frequent and sharp contractions in the economy; and the second between 1946 and 1980, when there was only one basic trend—up.

During the first era the planners of GM held the belief that the future was unpredictable. Sloan himself said that "we could not control the environment or predict its changes." But during the second era this philosophy was turned on its head. Panics or depressions were "outlawed" by an aggressive Government policy of control or stimulation. An attempt was made to create a "corporate Garden of Eden" in order to protect business from the natural gyrations of markets and the "evil forces of nature." With the backing of a Government statistocracy, with scientific consumer surveys, and with highly computerized planning departments to sort out all the data, management believed it had finally licked the business cycle. To put it simply, management assumed that the future was largely predictable.

Precisely at a time when the auto industry faced one of the

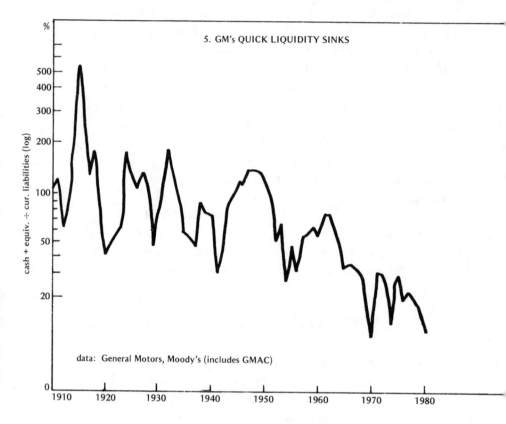

5. GM's QUICK LIQUIDITY SINKS

data: General Motors, Moody's (includes GMAC)

greatest challenges of its eighty-year history, the cash liquidity of General Motors—a measure of its ability to meet that challenge—was allowed to deteriorate to the levels approaching the *lowest* in history. On combining the balance sheets of GM and its captive finance subsidiary—General Motors Acceptance Corporation—we find that as of the end of 1979 cash liquidity had plunged from the 1970 crisis year of 47 percent to 19 percent. By mid-1980 the company had less than 12 cents in cash to meet every dollar in current debts. *Whereas General Motors had managed to turn a profit in the depths of the Great Depression of the 1930s, in 1980—still not far from the peak of the greatest boom ever—it announced record losses.*

I was putting the final touches on this chapter when a friend dropped in for an unexpected visit, a finger-poking, shoulder-shrugging skeptic of statistics, charts, or anything that looks too technical or academic. "Look at this," I said. "Unless they make a sudden-about face, they could soon be deep in trouble."

"Aren't you forgetting something?" he retorted.

"Like what, for example?"

"Like the men at the top, the guys who run GM. You think they're blind? You think they don't know what's going on? You have the gall to think that these little ratios of yours are everything? Those guys in there are *smart*. They are very knowledgeable. Their models probably have your data inputs plus much *more*. They've made mistakes, sure. Chrysler is a case in point. But most of them know what they're doing and you'd better believe it!"

He went on to make a convincing argument about what he called the "ultramodern control systems of business corporations" —controls over inventory, cash, quality, costs; even controls over controls; controls that had been primitive at best in the first half of the century.

To a degree he was right. Because of structural and technological advances, direct comparisons with previous panics and crashes have to be made with caution. However, these advances in themselves were insufficient to overcome basic weaknesses in the structure of the decision-making process, labor-management relations, labor productivity, and the quality of the final product.

Institutionalized Optimism

In addition to its own experts GM occasionally used outside consumer economists like Al Sindlinger. I first met Al in 1969, and I must say I was impressed. His computer selects a representative sample of households, and the names are then delivered to a staff of phone operators. The phone operators reach 1,300 households every week. The answers are fed right back into the computer, which prints out the data in the form of tables and graphs.

At first, General Motors was skeptical; but when the gunslingers saw it working, they must have been overjoyed. Imagine yourself in their shoes. For some time now you've been "sure" the trend is up, but that was only the *general* trend. Now you think you know, with a high degree of probability, what the *minor* fluctuations should be.

I asked Sindlinger if he had ever tested out his "consumer confidence index" during a deep and rapid business decline.

"That's an unknown element," he answered. "We only began taking these polls in 1956, and, since then, the basic trend, I must admit, has been up. Whether it will work as well in a bust as it does in a boom is a question that still needs to be tested."

As it turned out, five years later, in 1974, Sindlinger's indices did work; he warned General Motors of an impending decline in consumer spending well ahead of time. What did not work was General Motors' decision-making process. GM refused to accept the full implications of the decline in consumer confidence; its thinking and habit patterns were still locked into the era of expansion. Predictions were acceptable only as long as they were optimistic, or only slightly pessimistic. When the general trend was sharply down, the predictions fell on deaf ears. The auto business tumbled. Later, the big buying spree of gas-guzzlers that swept the country in 1977 and 1978 temporarily saved the day, but it did not stop the fundamental deterioration of the auto market.

In 1979 Al warned them again. He told them the whole auto business was going bad, that the big crunch was coming. He advised them to build up cash rapidly. "Don't be like the *Titanic,*" was his basic message. But by this time Sindlinger had been hammering away about the dangers of consumer-credit buying for many months, and the GM staff began to feel that the more Sindlinger talked gloom and doom, the more money they made. They gave him the old "cry wolf" treatment. What they didn't seem to understand was that Mr. Wolf, disguised as a Red Riding Hood, had been stalking the sheep all along. The consumer buying spree was masking a deep-down deterioration in consumer sentiment.

You'd think that once the wolf finally showed his real fangs—as he did in the first months of 1980—management would have changed their tune. Instead, they did precisely the opposite. The problem, as they perceived it, was not a fundamental deterioration in the auto market but primarily a change of tastes toward the small, fuel-efficient cars. The enemy, in their view, was not their own unbridled plunge into illiquidity. It was, rather, the uninhibited invasion of U.S. auto markets by the Japanese. In the first quarter of 1980 the signs of disaster were clear. A meager 12 percent drop in GM sales caused a whopping 87 percent decline in net income. Thus, by mid-June, with sales declines of 24 percent, it must have been quite obvious to management that they were headed for a sea of red ink. Nevertheless, their basic strategy remained unchanged: use the slump as an opportunity to expand market share; cut costs only *after* sales declines have been confirmed; boost capital spending in the face of big losses; aim for the future recovery of the auto market over the valley.

Chairman Estes's pep talk to kick off a major tent sale in May 1980 is a good illustration. He predicted that consumer confidence would perk up and increased sales would soon follow because of pent-up demand. Temporarily this might occur. Yet he did not mention the pent-up *supply:* a record eighty-three days of new car inventories in the hands of dealers, and as many as thirty million anxious-to-be-gotten-rid-of high-cost cars in the hands of consumers, and, most important, the capacity of domestic and foreign manufacturers to churn out a never ending stream of new automobiles.

Why was General Motors taking such an optimistic view of the future? One reason is because, had they been more realistic, they would have found themselves amputating very large segments of their plant and equipment and causing heavy premeditated losses. Why would cutbacks in operations result in immediate losses? The answer is obvious.

High Fixed Costs

Management was not too happy about the erosion of profit margins from 6.7 percent in 1973 to 4.4 percent in 1979. But they were unable to do much to stop it.

In 1973 interest costs at GM and its subsidiaries represented 36 cents of every dollar of net profit. In 1979 those interest costs were ninety-three cents of every dollar of net profit. In other words, the cost of borrowing money in 1979 was almost equivalent to the money earned.

On a per-unit basis the greatest fixed cost stemmed from declining labor productivity. But major attempts to improve productivity often boomeranged. For example, at the new Vega plant in Lordstown, Ohio, GM experimented with computers that controlled robot welding machines, subassembly areas, conveyor belts, and even quality control. The plant was, as "Adam Smith" described it in his book *Supermoney*, like "an iron-and-steel tropical rain forest, with the electric drills screaming like parakeets and the Unimat robot welders bending over the Vegas like big motor birds." Eventually this might lead to improvement in productivity, but in the first years it had precisely the opposite effect.

A new cost-cutting program was launched, and several hundred workers were laid off without the corresponding production cuts. Due to the accelerated schedules workers were squeezed even further. One woman complained: "I no sooner get one job done than I have to do another. I don't even have time to get a drink of water." GM got more production, all right. The only problem was that more and more Vegas began coming off the assembly line incomplete or damaged, and the repair yards became so cluttered with faultily built cars that the assembly line had to be shut down until the flaws were corrected. Finally the plant was shut down by a walkout. When the strike was settled weeks later, the corporation had incurred a loss of thousands of Vegas in production. On the surface the grievances of the workers were settled. Later, however, far more serious problems overflowed from the outside world onto the factory floor.

Although GM apparently did not have as much trouble as Ford, Ford's Mahwah plant in New Jersey was a good illustration of some of the difficulties that hit most of the industry in the 1970s. The *Wall Street Journal* of June 16, 1980, reports how in late 1974 Ford began producing its Granada sedan at the Mahwah plant, but the front end was so far out of alignment that Ford had to set up circus tents in the parking lot to repair the hundreds of cars involved. In mid-1975 a tough new assistant plant manager at Mahwah got good results. But his methods, which included heavy use of disciplinary procedures, created instant antagonisms. Workers took a strike vote that passed by 95 percent, and the union was set to walk out, ostensibly over health and safety issues. Management turnover then became a problem. Between 1975 and 1980 Mahwah saw four different plant managers, four assistant managers, and three quality-control managers. One wanted low costs, one wanted high quality, the next wanted a spotless plant. There wasn't any continuity.

As in many automobile assembly plants, boredom also took its toll, and some workers turned to drugs: According to one auto worker, "You could walk through certain parts of the body shop during the night shift and get high from just breathing." The result was "a lot of garbage coming out of the body shop."

In 1978 and 1979, according to the *Wall Street Journal,* the troubles reached a climax. A theft ring, which included security personnel, had been driving a truck into the plant at night, loading it with parts such as radios and electric motors for power windows, and driving out. Vandalism, meanwhile, was common. Some workers would get upset over something, and they would take a heavy metal drift pin and drive it right through the trunk or hood. In mid-1979, when truck production was closed down, the effect was traumatic. Workers who had been building trucks all their lives had to switch to the car-assembly line; and older men who couldn't handle their new jobs took medical leaves attributable primarily to psychological problems. Absenteeism soared, forcing managers to switch around workers on a day-to-day basis to fill gaps. Results were often disastrous. In one case they had to take a man who was a door-fitter and transform him into a quality-control inspector. The poor man had trouble speaking and writing proper English, a problem he solved by approving everything. One fellow worker recounted how "at first, they were going to have the guy inspect on a line where clutch assemblies and brake housings were installed, but someone said he will pass things that will get somebody killed. God knows what got by."

The Shift to Small Cars

Management in the entire industry often complained that the cost of safety, equal employment, and antipollution measures legislated by the Government, were taking a big slice out of profit margins. However, the most devastating cost for the automobile industry in 1980 was none of these. It comprised the massive expenditures being made in the mad race to convert production facilities, in order to meet the sudden demand for smaller cars.

GM, with a 62 percent share of the market, felt confident that, despite record losses, the right strategy was to *boost* the capital expenditures for the four-year period from 1980 to 1984 to $40 billion from a previous five-year forecast of $38 billion. Reason: Chairman Estes was still counting on a 17-million U.S. car market in 1982—almost the same figure that had been forecast years earlier for 1980. In October 1974, two weeks before the big drop in auto sales, GM's chairman, Richard C. Gerstenberg, was still predicting that the demand for cars would continue to expand, that more families would buy second cars, and that by 1980 the industry would be selling 17.5 million cars and trucks. He was wrong. Total U.S. auto and truck sales in 1979, *including imports,* reached only 14.1 million and, in the first half of 1980, were running at an annual rate of approximately 12 million. Mr. Gerstenberg's forecast was off by 31 percent! Despite a temporary recovery in mid-1980, there was little realistic hope that the forecast by Mr. Estes would do much better. There were, in fact, clear signs that, by the time General Motors and other auto giants managed to flood the market with small models, customers would no longer be interested, whether the cars were large, medium, or small.

The Auto Credit Balloon

GM earnings did not come from big profit margins but from big *volume.* Much of this large volume in turn was supported not by real demand, but by unprecedented injections of automobile credit. I divided the amount of net new auto credit created in the U.S.

every month by the number of new automobile registrations and noticed a rather startling pattern: Throughout the 1960s it never took more than $600 in new auto credit to generate each auto registration, and often took much less. But, in 1978, this had ballooned to $1,786. Looking at it in terms of accumulated figures, by 1980 there were approximately 40 million cars on the roads of America accounting for the bulk of the $115 billion in auto credit outstanding. That came to an average of an estimated $2, 875 in debt per car. Even if you average in the cars that were 100 percent paid up, there was $900 in debt overhanging every car registered in America, some 1.7 times as much as in 1974.

The Carter Administration's brief flirtation with credit controls in the second quarter of 1980 brought home the significance of this statistic: no credit = no sales. General Motors was vividly aware of this fact of life. What they did not yet know as of mid-1980 was the rest of the equation: attempts to restimulate credit creation = inflation fears = bond-market collapse = no credit. They were also unaware of the fact that the greatest danger facing the automobile industry was the possible effects of a paralysis in the conglomeration of banks, credit unions, and finance companies that supplied credit to consumers, dealers, and practically everyone involved in the buying and selling of cars.

The first to get caught in the automobile credit pyramid were the dealers. During the crunch in the summer of 1974 dealers around the country lamented the loss of up to 50 percent of potential sales because banks suddenly wanted at least 25 percent in down payments instead of the usual 10 or 15 percent, or because they wouldn't approve the financing at all. During the 1980 crunch many dealers were put out of business. *Automotive News* estimated that the auto industry lost 672 car dealers in 1979 alone versus a total of 402 in the three-year period from 1976 to 1978. In the first six months of 1980 approximately 600 dealers had closed. The head of the National Auto Dealers Association warned that one out of every four dealers could go under unless their financial squeeze was eased.

General Motors, the largest manufacturer in the world, was on a collision course with bankruptcy. In order to veer from this course the company would have to build up a large cash position; phase out large-car production almost entirely; and cut back sharply on investments in *both* small and large-car productive facilities—in short, follow the example of their predecessors of the early 1930s. Would GM take these steps in time? If they did not, what changes might eventually be in store for the U.S. auto industry, the combustion engine, and transportation in general? Only time would tell.

3

The
Utilities

IT WAS GENERALLY ASSUMED that American Telephone &
Telegraph was recession-proof. By 1979 there were 140 million
telephones, used by over 70 million faithful customers making 135
million calls and paying an average bill of over $600 month after
month. The company was not, however, invulnerable to the Great
Money Panic. The reasons are fourfold.

First, management, much like that of General Motors, tended to
be overconfident. Blaming inflation, AT&T reported that earnings
in the first quarter of 1980 rose by only 7 percent, the smallest gain
in eight years, and as its chairman admitted, that "1980 would be a
particularly tough year." Nevertheless, the company still went full
steam ahead with its plans to raise construction spending for the
year to $16.9 billion, $200 million more than previously announced, and up $1.1 billion from the previous year. The company
hoped to raise about two-thirds of the money from internal
sources, leaving about $7 billion to be raised in money markets,
most of it through long-term debentures—admittedly an "un-
happy prospect in the face of current interest costs."

Second, in a sharp business decline accompanied by acute cash shortages, telephone services could become one of the first targets of cost-cutting by business, Government institutions, and households. Long-distance calls were particularly vulnerable. Before the superboom took off in 1976, long-distance calls were almost equal in dollar volume to the revenues received from local service, both being slightly under $14 billion. By 1980, after four years of easy money, expansive corporate budgets, and more liberal attitudes toward the use of long-distance calls, toll revenues rose 10 percent, or $3⅛ billion, above local service revenue. In short, as much as 60 percent of AT&T's profits came from a service that could drop considerably in a major business setback.

The third reason Ma Bell was headed for trouble was rooted in the problem of fixed plant and equipment costs. I picked up a 1979 annual report and divided the number of telephones in operation into total plant and equipment (before depreciation). I was surprised to discover that each and every phone required approximately $884 worth of equipment and plant to back it up. As long as customers kept their phones, there was no problem. But as soon as companies and families made the necessary decision to discontinue their phone extensions or, worse yet, do without a specific line entirely, AT&T would be left holding the bag with billions of dollars of underused or temporarily useless equipment. If faced with the alternative of either accepting massive delinquencies in bill payments or cutting off service—either a temporary cutoff of income or a more permanent loss of business—Ma Bell might very well prefer the former. In either case, cash inflows were bound to drop sharply.

The fourth and by far the most compelling reason AT&T was vulnerable to the Great Money Panic was the overwhelming burden of fixed interest charges. Imagine four states the size of Texas, side by side, sprawling over into the Rocky Mountains, the Gulf, and Northern Mexico. Now do the same for Illinois, New York, and California. Finally, put them all together and calculate the total interest paid on their combined debt. When you get the answer, compare it to the interest expense at Ma Bell in one year, and you will discover that, surprisingly, Ma Bell still pays slightly

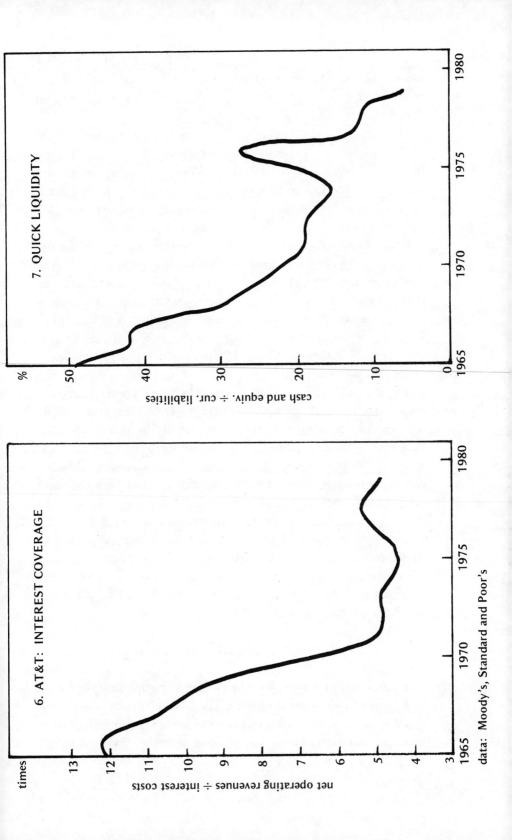

6. AT&T: INTEREST COVERAGE

times

net operating revenues ÷ interest costs

7. QUICK LIQUIDITY

%

cash and equiv. ÷ cur. liabilities

data: Moody's, Standard and Poor's

more. The reason is quite obvious: the company has a total debt of some $44 billion—approximately equivalent to the total national debt of West Germany or France.

Of course, absolute amounts, no matter how impressive, are not as meaningful as the ratios—relative measures that account for the fact that Ma Bell is, after all, the world's biggest company in total assets. The ratios show that since 1954, when mid-century expansionist fever first overcame the company, the liquidity of AT&T has fallen sharply.

Graph 6 on page 31 shows AT&T's "interest coverage." Basically it answers the question: Assuming no other expenses, how many times over can they pay interest costs with net operating revenues (the amount left over after meeting operating costs and before paying income taxes)? In 1965 net operating revenues were sufficient to cover interest charges nearly twelve times. By July 1980 they plummeted to *only 4.9 times.* Later, during the Great Money Panic, credit-rating agencies such as Moody's or Standard and Poor's might be forced to downgrade AT&T bonds from their traditional triple-A rating. It would then become increasingly difficult for the company to raise money in the marketplace. In that event, liquidity ratios would decline still further, making investors still more skeptical and thereby compounding AT&T's money problems, an uprecedented vicious circle which could spread throughout the industry. Graph 7 on page 31, showing AT&T's quick liquidity, confirms this conclusion. In 1965 AT&T had enough in cash and equivalent assets to cover 49 percent of its short-term debt. At the beginning of 1979 it could cover only 6.8 percent.

AT&T was bound to be burdened with these debts for many years to come.

New Con Eds In The Making

When Con Edison shocked the investment community by omitting a quarterly dividend in early 1974, the company was on the brink of bankruptcy. A combination of high rates, meter reading mix-ups, and messy bill collections had prompted irate customers to slow down their payments. The company wrote off $41 million in noncollectible receivables—65 percent greater than in 1973. Plant breakdowns were commonplace. Quick liquidity plunged to a new low of 4.3 percent; interest coverage fell to 2.0 times, one of the lowest reported for any major electric utility at the time. As a result, utility companies were practically locked out of the bond markets.

It was precisely when things looked the darkest that there was an improvement ahead. By setting up a comptroller's office and establishing controls in every direction, cost overruns were cut drastically. Innovative bill collection systems were put into effect, reducing unpaid revenue days to thirty-two from a high of fifty-nine in 1973. Most important, the State of New York came to the rescue with $612 million and bought two burdensome power plants from Con Ed. The end results were dramatic. Cash liquidity soared to 90 percent and interest coverage reached 2.8 times. By 1979 the New York utility had so much cash that it could afford to turn down offers from Wall Street investment bankers for an extra $100 million in long-term financing. To be sure, long-term earnings prospects were questionable. Electric kilowatt use was declining as more New Yorkers conserved electricity, and the common stock was locked in a downward trend. Nevertheless, the company stood out as one of the few that had undergone a preliminary housecleaning and now had a fighting chance to survive a liquidity crunch.

Unfortunately, the same could not be said for most utilities. By the end of 1979 *over half of the nation's top ten electric utilities were worse off financially than Con Edison was in 1973.* Seven of the top ten had lower interest coverage, with Southern Company, American Electric Power, Consolidated Edison, Philadelphia Electric, Detroit Edison, Commonwealth Edison, and Virginia Power & Electric plunging or remaining below the landmark 2.0 level. Five of the top ten had considerably worse liquidity. For example, in 1979 Southern California Edison and Detroit Edison had almost nine times *less* cash liquidity than Con Ed in 1973, while Virginia Power & Electric, believe it or not, had over four thousand times less liquidity.

TABLE 2

The Liquidity of America's Top Ten Utilities

Cash and equivalent as a percent of short-term debts				
Liquidity Rank	Company	1979	1974	1970
1	Consolidated Edison	68.2	12.0	9.1
2	Southern Co.	18.9	4.6	22.5
3	Am. Elec. Power	10.5	14.7	12.2
4	Philadelphia Electric	9.8	3.9	10.2
5	Pacific Gas & Electric	7.6	14.4	7.8
6	Commonwealth Edison	2.7	5.6	9.2
7	Public Service Gas & Elec.	1.6	6.0	17.8
8	So. Calif. Edison	0.5	19.3	6.0
9	Detroit Edison	0.4	5.1	5.4
10	Virginia Power & Electric	0.001	1.2	4.1

Consolidated Edison in 1973: 4.3

Data: Annual reports

TABLE 3

Interest Coverage of America's Top Ten Utilities

Net Income Before Income Taxes Divided by Interest Costs				
Interest-Coverage Rank	Company	1979	1974	1970
1	Public Service Gas & Elec.	2.9	1.9	2.2
2	So. Calif. Edison	2.4	3.7	2.8
3	Pacific Gas & Electric	2.0	2.5	3.3
4	Virginia Power & Electric	1.8	1.4	2.5
5	Detroit Edison	1.8	1.7	2.6
6	Am. Elec. Power	1.8	1.1	1.8
7	Consolidated Edison	1.8	2.0	2.2
8	Southern Co.	1.6	1.4	3.1
9	Philadelphia Electric	1.6	1.7	0.7
10	Commonwealth Edison	1.4	4.1	4.5

Data: Moody's Utility

When we compare interest coverage with liquidity, we see an interesting pattern. Most electric utilities were at best able to trade off long-term financial weaknesses for short-term strengths, or vice versa. Consolidated Edison was able to improve its cash liquidity ratio from 12.0 percent to 68.2 percent, but its interest coverage, meanwhile, declined from 2.0 to 1.8 in the same period. Southern California Edison was able to reduce the burden of interest costs considerably, but, in the process, it chucked away all of its cash as its liquidity plunged from 19.3 percent in 1974 to 0.5 percent in 1979. By examining both measures, therefore, the conclusion is obvious: the industry as a whole was far worse off in 1979 than in 1974.

How did the utilities get themselves into this kind of bind? Would it be possible to restore their financial health merely with rate hikes? Or was a full-scale cleanout needed? Let's take a closer look at Detroit's Commonwealth Edison (Com Ed).

With a pioneering spirit, Thomas G. Ayers, chairman of Commonwealth Edison, thrust his firm into the forefront of nuclear power plant construction. The Arab oil embargo and his growing conviction that energy shortages were "here to stay" prompted him to embark upon a new set of projects with a total cost of $4.6 billion from 1977 to 1981. The underlying rationale made sense: "Jump into the future ahead of the other utilities. Put the big engineering and construction costs behind you by spending more now. Develop the ability to produce cheap energy, big savings for customers, and high earnings for stockholders in the years to come."

The timing, however, couldn't have been worse. Commonwealth Edison's cash liquidity had declined steadily from 1965, and by 1979 it was some 50 percent lower than in 1974. The drop in Com Ed's interest coverage was even more precipitous. In the mid-sixties a four-year testing phase was completed for the prototype of a new 200-megawatt nuclear generator, and Ayers was "sure he had a winner." From that point on nuclear plant construction literally took off. The resulting acceleration of borrowing in the money markets, coupled with a new era of higher interest costs, caused Commonwealth Edison's interest coverage to collapse from a high of 4.8 in 1965 to a low of 1.4 in 1979.

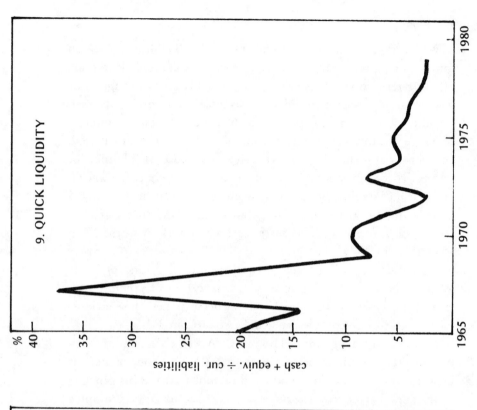

8. COMMONWEALTH EDISON: INTEREST COVERAGE

times

net operating revenues ÷ interest costs

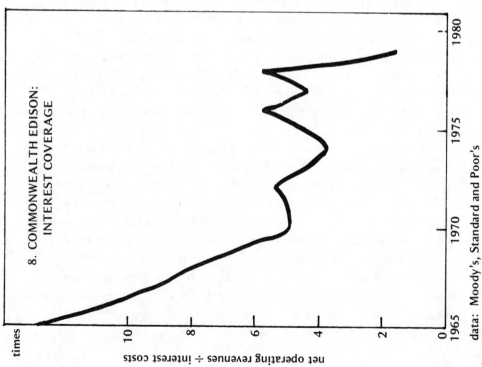

9. QUICK LIQUIDITY

%

cash + equiv. ÷ cur. liabilities

data: Moody's, Standard and Poor's

Yes, New York's Con Ed was saved by New York State. But who was going to help the *new* Con Ed's speeding toward a collision with a money panic?

The Squeeze on Revenues

The illiquidity of the electric utilities would not have presented a great problem if only their revenues could be guaranteed. Even before the money panic, however, the growth rate in residential power consumption began to decline sharply. Based on data from the Edison Electric Institute, I have calculated that, between 1946 and 1970, the yearly growth rate in kilowatt hours used per residential customer tended to remain above 5 percent. By the mid-sixties industry analysts noticed a slight softening trend, but any concerns they possibly had were forgotten with a new upsurge that began in 1968. Most assumed that energy needs would continue to

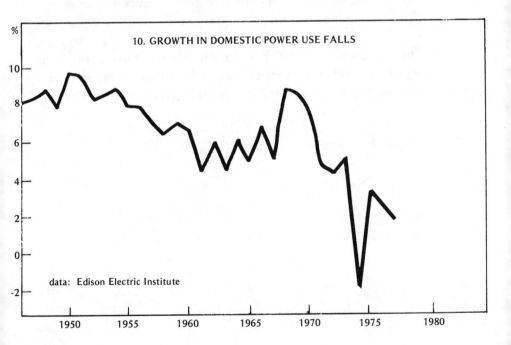

10. GROWTH IN DOMESTIC POWER USE FALLS

data: Edison Electric Institute

grow at approximately the same pace until the year 2000, and they projected residential energy demands based primarily on this assumption.

In 1970 the growth began to slow. Then, in 1974, largely due to spiraling energy costs, electric utility customers actually cut back on their use of electricity. The last time something like that took place was at the very bottom of the depression in 1933; and even then the decline was only two-tenths of 1 percent, from 601 kwh. to 600 kwh. This time the average household reduced its electricity consumption by *2.1 percent!* The obvious cause was the energy crisis, forcing the average bill up sharply at a time when disposable income was being hurt by the recession. But, as this graph clearly shows, the slowdown of the growth rate actually began in 1970, three years *before* the Arab oil embargo.

The implications were far-reaching. Continual inputs of large doses of money and energy had provided a springboard for the great success of the American power companies and had been the two driving forces behind the twentieth-century economic machine. Assuming a continuation in this growth, the utilities made two basic errors. First, they overlooked the fact that there *are* limits to growth—semipermeable barriers that force a temporary retreat. Second, they allowed their debt commitments to stretch well *beyond* those limits. A major cash squeeze was unavoidable.

4

Retailers:
Caught in
the Revolving Door

WHEN FOOD FAIR FILED for bankruptcy under Chapter 11 early in October 1978, it came as a surprise to many analysts. *Value Line,* for example, had reported only a few weeks earlier: "In our opinion, management's consolidation policy is sound and will soon begin to contribute to improved results at the grocery store division." And only a few months before that, Food Fair's president Friedland spoke of "new merchandising and sales programs that have produced excellent sales increases." It wasn't the first time retail analysts were caught by surprise. A & P, once the number one supermarket chain, was periodically shaken by tight money, knocked around by fierce competition from chains with more up-to-date merchandising methods, and finally taken over by the West German Tengelmann Group. Grand Union and Korvettes, not far behind, were kept afloat only by the money injections from similar foreign groups.

For many years it was believed that these casualties were merely the natural consequences of free competitive enterprise. But by the late 1970s many retailers began to wonder if there wasn't more to it than that; they smelled something fishy in the consumer-credit buying spree. Federated Department Stores led the skeptical re- tailers by embarking in 1978 on a tough cost-cutting and inventory- trimming campaign. J. C. Penney at first attempted the opposite course with a sales blitzkrieg and a 54 percent inventory buildup, but by 1979 they also were forced to slash inventories to levels considered safe in the event of a recession.

Nevertheless, there was little effort to reduce the industry's dependence on credit. Between 1974 and 1978 retail sales increased from $480 billion to $652 billion, for a growth rate of 9 percent annually. In the same period new consumer credit increased from $9.6 billion to $44.8 billion for an average rate of growth of almost 92 percent a year—*ten times faster than the growth in sales.* Furthermore, it took only six cents in new consumer credit to generate every dollar of sales increase in 1974. It took *twenty-six cents* to accomplish the same results in 1978.

What happened? Where did the extra credit money go? Some of it went into the defense sector. Much of it wound up overseas in the Eurodollar and Eurocurrency markets. But most of the extra credit apparently was wasted on inefficient projects, which by this time had almost become the trademark of the American economy. There remained only one sensible solution—a reduction in Gov- ernment and consumer spending and waste, together with an improvement in worker productivity and a stronger dollar. Unfor- tunately, the primary concern of businessmen and political leaders was not to rebuild the economic machine. Rather, most sought to apply more cosmetics and open the money-and-credit valves still further. One reason the latter alternative was chosen is now evident: *Unlike previous periods, retailers and wholesalers could no longer withstand the shock of a contraction in consumer spending.*

Table 4 shows the rapid deterioration in the liquidity of the top ten U.S. retail companies in the 1970s. As of the end of fiscal 1979 *every one, without exception, showed worse cash positions than in 1974.* K-Mart's cash liquidity, although relatively better than the rest, had fallen almost in half. Federated Department Stores let their liquidity dip from 8.6 percent in 1974 to 2.5 percent in 1979.

TABLE 4
The Liquidity of America's Top Ten Retailers

			Cash and equivalent as a percent of short-term liabilities		
Liquidity Rank	Sales Rank	Company	1979	1974	1970
1	3	K Mart	13.9	25.4	13.0
2	2	Safeway	9.1	12.1	21.4
3	7	A & P	8.4	12.8	35.2
4	5	Kroger	8.1	13.1	19.3
5	9	Rapid American	6.6	14.4	39.3
6	10	May Dept. Stores	6.0	9.6	21.0
7	1	Sears Roebuck	3.8	3.9	6.1
8	4	J.C. Penney	3.2	5.8	17.6
9	8	Federated Dept. Stores	2.5	8.6	17.5
10	6	Woolworth	2.2	18.4	14.6

Woolworth, meanwhile, permitted its liquidity to plunge to one-eighth of the level reached during the previous credit crisis.

Many of the short-term liabilities were in commercial paper, and the biggest of the commercial paper users among the retailers was Sears, Roebuck (via its captive finance subsidiary), borrowing about $3 billion by 1980. As the number one retailer in sales volume it was assumed to be the most reliable borrower. Yet behind the facade of strength management was in turmoil. In 1978 they made an unexpected shift from a high-price strategy to a high-discount strategy in order to compete aggressively with other large retailers. Then, in 1979, the company made another 180-degree turn back to high-priced merchandise.

Sears' greatest vulnerability stemmed from its deep involvement in the money business through its subsidiary, All State Insurance, which had been producing some 40 percent of Sears' net income, as compared with only 18 percent during the previous business peak. This helped disguise the fact that Sears' profit margin on retail sales had declined from 4½ percent in 1973 to approximately 2 percent in 1978. Sears was deeply involved in the money business in another way, the financing of customer charge accounts. Throughout the 1950s and 1960s the bulk of the accounts were in installment credit on big ticket items. Later, Sears became the leader in a major shift to "revolving credit." The customer liked the arrangement because he had the option to roll over his account continually on a perpetual basis, paying a minimum portion of his outstanding balance. And Sears liked it because it attracted a broader spectrum of the public and brought in an extra bonus in the form of interest-related profits. Unfortunately, the reliability of the revolving credit generally did not match that of the installment credit. Consequently, the quality of their receivables declined, while the quantity increased. Sears became one of the largest consumer banks in the U.S., owning approximately 25 percent of the $30 billion in receivables outstanding in the retail trade. All fine and dandy—until interest rates began to soar.

Unfortunately, few industry leaders became concerned about the revolving-credit, commercial-paper trap until it was too late. By early 1980 the nation's three largest retailers—Sears, Roebuck, Montgomery Ward, and J. C. Penney—were in the throes of one of the worst sales declines in their history, "admittedly due as much to internal management problems as they were due to the rapidly deteriorating economy," as the *New York Times* stated the case in its June 11, 1980, issue. According to Monroe H. Greenstein, a principal of Bear, Stearns & Company, Sears upgraded too much and chopped off its low-end customers; Penney's was having trouble concentrating on more than one thing at a time; and Montgomery Ward was having the most trouble of all, upgrading at a time when its private labels were losing impact. All three retailers suffered from the poor timing of major marketing decisions, a lack of flexibility in merchandising plans, and weak internal communications that delayed response time to changing conditions. All three erred when they sought to combat the erosion of their profit margins, brought on by rising costs, by injecting a higher percentage of more profitable, higher-priced goods into their traditional lines. Most important, all three were overdependent on the consumer debt pyramid. Although the initial trauma of federal credit tightening in April and May of 1980 was eased temporarily, the big shock was yet to come.

5

Where Banks Get Their Money

THE TIME IS June 1980, the place, your local bank. You walk in to make a deposit. No big deal. Just the same old fill-out-the-slip-wait-on-line routine. Out of the corner of your eye you notice the security guard leaning against one of the counters and staring blankly at the tellers. When was the last time you went to the bank and didn't notice the security guard? You spot the faithful TV camera and visualize how it would be set into motion by the flick of a switch. You read the good old FDIC sign:

DEPOSITS INSURED UP TO $100,000
FEDERAL DEPOSIT INSURANCE CORPORATION

By the time you hand the money to the teller, you feel assured that nothing can go wrong; that the money will be there when you need it; and that it's backed by the Government, the police, and, indirectly at least, by all the authority and power of the world. You assume your money is safe. But how safe is it, you might ask.

If your bank was like the majority of banks in the United States in June 1980, it had the lowest liquidity of the twentieth century. And if it was illiquid, there was a very good chance you might not be able to get your money back precisely when you needed it the most.

"Why?" you ask. "Do you mean to say there could be another bank holiday? What about the FDIC? What about the Federal Reserve?"

Unfortunately, the Federal Deposit Insurance Corporation was little more than just that, an insurance corporation that had a little over $9.8 billion in resources (plus an additional $3 billion drawing permitted from the U.S. Treasury) to cover $1.2 trillion in deposits at the commercial banks. This represented slightly better than one cent in insurance money for every dollar of deposits.

"Only one cent?"

"Right, only one cent!"

But the inadequacies of the FDIC were really not the main problem. The main problem was that most commercial banks, in particular the large, respectable city banks, were speculating, that is, wheeling and dealing.

"That's just doomsday science fiction," you say. "You must be exaggerating." But the main reason you react that way is because banking and high finance were almost always hidden behind a cloud of mystery and technical jargon. If you could take a trip physically through the vaults and computers and follow one of your dollars on its trajectory throughout the banking system, you might take a different view.

Hypothetically we assume that one particular dollar is a typical dollar in a typical bank. We give it a fixed identity and call it "D.D." (initials for Deposit Dollar). We hand D.D. over to the teller. The last time D.D. got plunked into a commercial bank was over two decades ago. Back in 1960 a middle-aged lady with horn-rimmed glasses and red tennis shoes deposited it into a passbook savings account. In those days the going was slow and easy. No hustle, no hassle. D.D. simply was sent off on a series of constructive jobs to only the most reliable borrowers with a reasonable assurance that it would be returned to the depositor whenever demanded or desired. But that was the old days.

Hot Money

In 1980 it's no joy ride. The first change in D.D.'s position is not in the bank's investment policies. It's the result of other deposit dollars. In 1960 D.D.'s companions were almost invariably easygoing rational dollars left with the banks for indefinite periods of time by families, businessmen, and other long-term savers. This time D.D. is thrown into the vaults with a new breed of deposits—jumpy, nervous, and haughty types, who pick up and leave at a moment's notice in the never ending search for higher interest rates. D.D. is thrown into a den of hot money, which includes, as *Business Week* has described it, "hot certificates of deposit that have been broker solicited and will go to the highest bidder, hotter short-term funds with maturities anywhere from a few days to a few months, and the hottest federal funds."

The first new group is the certificate of deposit (CD), finicky and haughty characters worth over $100,000 each, who refuse to stay for more than thirty to ninety days at a time, and are constantly threatening to take off to some other area unless they're given a better deal. Then there are Eurodollars, American dollars that years back got marched off to London, Switzerland, Germany, Singapore, or the Bahamas and have now come back warning they're "not gonna stick around for long." The last and hottest group are the federal funds—bank reserves loaned out daily from banks with surpluses to banks with deficits. Most of the federal funds are actually just "country-bumpkin dollars conned into big city schemes and shenanigans." The conservative country banks send them to the big city banks scurrying for the best bid, with small-town people believing all their money is still back home in the good old country banks. As if CDs, Eurodollars, and federal funds are not enough to endanger the banking system, there is also a gang of dollars sneaking in through the back door that don't even get counted as deposits—commercial paper.

In 1980 these strange newcomers covered 45 percent of all investments and loans at the reporting member banks. Back in 1970 it was only 19 percent; in 1966, 12 percent; and in 1946, virtually nonexistent. The banks have changed indeed.

"What's so bad about these new instruments?" you ask. Well, it all boils down to a question of stability and reliability. CD deposits were not dependable because the owners were normally sophisticated individuals ready to switch into higher yielding media at a moment's notice, deposits some bankers call "wild card money." Federal funds were potentially questionable because, according to Lester Gable, vice-president of the Minneapolis Fed, any reverse flow would very likely "produce chaotic effects today or tomorrow. Fed funds are now being traded like marbles, and some day banks might be lending funds to the wrong banks at the wrong time." Commercial paper was dangerous because, according to one analyst at Standard and Poor's, such borrowing by the holding company created "a double leveraging." They were used like deposits, but were not backed by the reserve requirements imposed by the Fed. In addition, commercial paper was often not shown on banks' balance sheets, and rarely appeared even as footnotes for the financial statements the banks publish in the financial press.

Suppose we let that deposit dollar to which we gave the identity "D.D." take over the scenario and tell us directly what happens once he starts on his journey from the teller's window. He is, at the outset, shocked by the nature of his traveling companions. Spotting an old friend in the crowd, he asks, "What is this, some kind of alien invasion or something?"

"Invasion?" answers his friend. "If you think this is bad, wait till you see the big New York money banks. That's where the CDs of $100,000 or over, plus federal funds, Eurodollars, commercial paper, and the rest make up 47 percent of all sources of money."

"Almost one of them for every one of us?"

"That's right. Incredible, isn't it?"

"But listen. As long as they don't bother us, as long as they mind their own business, what do we have to worry about? We're segregated from them in the bank's accounts, aren't we?"

"Are you kidding? Look what happened to Franklin National. All of a sudden the owners of the CDs, federal funds, and such decided not to renew, and a bunch of characters like the ones you see here flew the coop. Most people thought it was just foreign currency speculation. But that was only the trigger. The real problems were the CDs, the Eurodollars, the federal funds, the commercial paper."

"So what? I mean, what do we care?"

"Are you blind or something? If it hadn't been for the Fed's big rescue operation, respectable passbook savings deposits like us would have been left there holding the bag."

"You mean really stuck?"

"Exactly! And the same could happen to us unless the Fed is able to come to the rescue. But personally I doubt they could possibly rescue more than one or two large banks at a time."

"You mean the bank doors would close? You mean we'd be locked in and the depositors locked out?"

The two are deep in their conversation when they notice the crowd of dollars pushing toward the elevator. It is the time of the day when all net inflows are sorted, counted, and marched upstairs. Department heads then make investment recommendations. The crowd pushes and shoves, and D.D. is squeezed toward the elevator. As the door closes, he catches a glimpse of his friend waving and gesturing as if to warn him of some unknown danger above, a danger far worse than the hot money crowd below.

The Chase Between the Fed and the Banks

As D.D. rides the packed elevator, he can't get his mind off the problem of hot money. "Why did the Federal Reserve let the banks do such a thing?" he wonders. Little does he know that it had been the Fed itself that had inadvertently forced the banks to change their practices.

In the fifties and early sixties the Federal Reserve did little more than lecture the banks once in a while: "Naughty, naughty, be good boys now." But it wasn't until 1966 that the Fed really became upset with the banks for dishing out so much money to the corporations and decided to do something about it. The drama began when the Federal Reserve allowed interest rates on Treasury bills and other investments to go up while freezing the rates banks could pay for their deposits. The Fed expected that, as a result of this strategy, the banks would no longer be able to bid competitively for deposits, and would therefore have less money available to loan out. The first part of the Fed's strategy worked very well, perhaps too well; CDs oozed out of the banks, dropping from $16 billion in 1968 to $5 billion by 1970.

The second half of the Fed's strategy—the part about cutting off loans to the big corporations—did not work so well. Rather than cut down on loans and forfeit profits, the whole banking industry veered from sound banking practices and moved into unknown and dangerous territory. That's when the banks came up with the gimmicks to raise new funds. Eurodollar borrowings by banks soared from approximately $15 billion in early 1968 to $30 billion in 1970. Federal-fund borrowings surged from $10 billion to $20 billion in the same period. Then these sources began to run dry, and the banks' holding companies printed commercial paper as though it were going out of style. Within nine months bank-related commercial paper outstanding doubled from a little under $4 billion to almost $8 billion.

Finally, in 1970 the Fed figured it was no use; they gave up trying to squeeze the banks. Several years later this "ugly game of chicken that the commercial banks and the Federal Reserve habitually play against each other" would resume, and the federal-fund rate would soar once again from 3 percent to 13 percent between 1972 and 1974. But at that time the Fed had enough and wanted interest rates down. The Penn Central crisis was scaring the daylights out of everyone, including businessmen, bankers, and Richard Nixon. So the Fed suddenly reversed the earlier strategy. It removed the lid on Regulation Q (maximum interest on savings) and allowed the banks a free hand in bidding for money.

It was the beginning of an aggressive policy of bank-loan stimulation. It was also the trigger for rampant inflation. Much later, in 1979, the Federal Reserve would become extremely concerned about the overextended positions of the banks. But, according to Business Week, "for all their concern today, the regulatory agencies not only permitted but actually encouraged the frantic growth of the past decade."

CD money soon flowed back to the banks like a torrent, jumping from the $5 billion low in 1960 to $90 billion by mid-July 1980. You'd think that with this kind of a bonanza the banks would have given up all the other gimmicks they learned to use during the 1968-70 squeeze and 1974-75 crunch. No such luck! They did cut down on Eurodollar borrowings somewhat, but bank-related commercial paper outstanding went from $8 billion at the end of 1970 to $22 billion by mid-July 1980. At first the hot money was readily available, and no one seemed to make much of it. But by 1979 banks were in "ferocious competition" for hot money to support all their loans. According to one bank officer, "this development not only makes banks vulnerable...but moves them a long way from their original mission in the economic life of the nation, which was to manage piled-up or assumed assets, the formal definition of 'banks.' The quality of the entire banking enterprise is deteriorating and the ice is getting thinner all the time."

In the middle of 1978 the introduction of the six-month money market certificate added further fuel to the fire; and by the spring of 1980, $380 billion of these certificates, representing 24 percent of all deposits in the banking system, were "waiting like ticking time bombs in banks and thrift institutions around the country," as William E. Donahue expressed it in the *New York Times* for May 11, 1980. But these were merely the inputs, the sources of money. Far greater risks were taken with the outputs—the loans and investments.

6

What the Banks Do with the Money

THE ELEVATOR COMES to a stop on the twentieth floor. D.D. is shoved out into the corridor and badly trampled in the stampede of hot money characters rushing to be first in line. They line up in front of a bank investment officer sitting behind a plain, metal desk at the end of the corridor. D.D. wonders why his friend was so upset; everything seems to be quite proper. He figures he'll be sent out to the Government as he was the last time, maybe a few inventory-financing jobs. That's quite normal, no problem there. The bank officer calls out the investment instructions to the crowd. "Fourteen cents for cash—eight cents for government securities— twelve cents for tax-exempt state and municipal bonds."

The hot money nods obediently, figuring it's a good paying job, so why not? But D.D. likes the relative safety of Treasury bills. It is obvious from the outset that investment policies of 1980 bankers are quite the opposite of those of the 1960s. He raises his voice in protest.

"Wait a minute," shouts D.D. "Only eight cents for government securities? What's the big idea? Last time I was here it was over thirty cents! Besides, from what I hear, the tax-exempt municipal bond market is in a shambles. Why are you throwing good money after bad?"

The man ignores the question and continues down the list. "Three cents for agency bonds—one cent for stocks and other securities—four cents for federal funds—fifteen cents for real estate and..."

"What?" D.D. interrupts once again. "Real estate? What kind of real estate?"

"About five cents for office and commercial construction, about seven cents for one-to-four family residences," the man answers.

"I don't get it. You mean you guys are still sinking money into offices and apartments when real estate is falling apart?"

The bank officer is visibly upset. He has no time to argue. "Two cents to brokers—two and a half cents to farmers." He pauses for a moment, glancing first at D.D. and then taking a deep breath to read off the rest in a single burst. "Two-cents-for-mobile-homes-and-appliances, six-cents-for-personal-loans, one-cent-for-home-improvement-loans, twenty-three-cents-to-commerce-and-industry, five-cents-for-auto-loans."

D.D. glares at the bank officer, and the bank officer glares back. The officer then reads off a long list of non-oil-producing LDCs (less developed countries): "Brazil, Peru, Zaire, etcetera, etcetera." D.D., not quite relishing the thought of his ashes being spread across the four corners of the Southern Hemisphere, begins to show visible signs of panic. "Everyone and his brother knows the less developed countries are sure to default this year or next! Have you gone bananas?"

"What are you griping about?" the banker asks after a long pause. "The man who deposited you is getting his interest, isn't he? So shut up and move on."

But he felt he had good reason to gripe. In 1960, for every dollar left on deposit in the nation's commercial banks and thrift institutions, at least thirty-seven cents remained in equity for depositors. In 1980 the situation was quite different. For every dollar deposited in the banking system (including s & l's and savings banks) ninety cents was loaned out and locked up in brick and mortar,

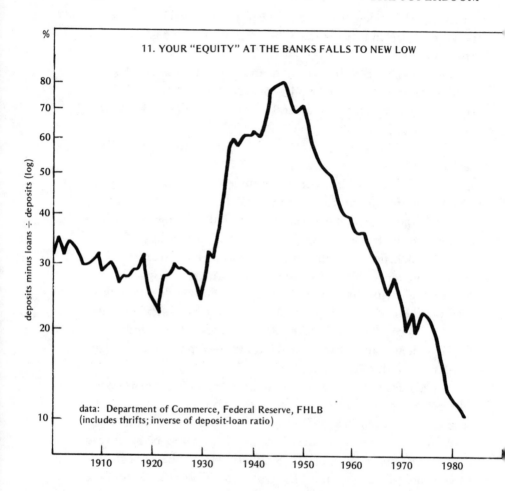

11. YOUR "EQUITY" AT THE BANKS FALLS TO NEW LOW

data: Department of Commerce, Federal Reserve, FHLB
(includes thrifts; inverse of deposit-loan ratio)

leaving only ten cents in equity. As illustrated in the accompanying graph, this ratio was lower than the low points reached immediately prior to the panics of 1904, 1907, 1914, 1920, 1929. It was also considerably lower than that of the credit crunch of 1974-75. *The 1980 ratio was by far the lowest and most vulnerable of the twentieth century.*

Perhaps D.D. wouldn't mind so much were the projects financed by the bank loans at least reasonable and solid. Instead, many of them bordered on the ridiculous. First, he is sent to the First

Pennsylvania Corporation in Philadelphia, where the head of this major bank uses him to speculate in over $1 billion in U.S. Government securities he plans to sell later at a higher price. However, the bonds fall sharply in value, so the bank takes a big loss of over $100 million in the second quarter of 1980. According to *Barron's,* "banks were willy-nilly...directing scarce credit from worthier borrowers [and] forfeiting their obligations as...custodians of other people's money." D.D. is then sent on a wild goose chase at Chrysler, a merry-go-round with a sinking retail company, and a narrow escape in the Hunt brothers' silver collapse. He wonders whether he'll ever make it back to the bank in one piece.

Speculation

As if this weren't enough, there was the speculation in foreign exchange, betting the dollar would go down or the deutschmark would go up, gambling for big stakes, making "big killings." No banker in his right mind talked much about it. They just did it, and if they did talk, they dared not mention the word speculation. "We're just hedging against anticipated fluctuations in our foreign currency loans," said the bank spokesmen.

It first began in a big way in the early seventies. Up until that time it was mostly the big multinational corporations that were involved in foreign-currency trading. They bought foreign currencies partly because of growing fears of a dollar devaluation, and the banks acted only as agents for these transactions, usually not getting directly involved as a principal. Then, in 1971 Nixon set the dollar loose, and some multinational corporations made big killings in German marks, Swiss francs, and Japanese yen. The bankers who were handling these transactions for them began to become envious; they didn't have a piece of the action. Thus, it wasn't long before the banks caught on and began doing it with their own money—or, rather, with the money entrusted to them by depositors. Almost all of the big city banks got into the act either directly or indirectly. Currency speculation was not an isolated or sporadic development; it was a systemic change that overcame the banks. Many banks did put limits on their foreign-exchange trading departments, but most were so pleased by the boost in earnings that they gave their traders a free hand and cheered them on from the sidelines. The foreign-currency traders soon became the big heroes, the white-haired boys who were wined, dined, and bonused all the way to the top.

But in 1973-74 the joy ride came to a screeching halt. The sure-shot, escape-from-the-dollar currencies took a flop. Down came the marks, the francs, the guilders, the schillings, and the yen. And down with them came the heyday of the boys in the banks' foreign-exchange departments. They got the blame for the Franklin National collapse, for the collapse of the West German Herstadt Bank, and for heavy losses in other banks. Under the headlines there would be a picture of this poor fellow from the foreign-exchange department who had committed all the sins and caused all the trouble. "Just a fool speculator," cried the bankers. "He did it to us, and here's his mug shot to prove his guilt." While he was making big killings in the markets it was "a hedge." Now that he took big losses, it was called "fool speculation." Okay. So they had their fling. By 1980 the trouble was all over, right? Not quite. The trouble had barely begun.

The speculation in foreign currencies at the banks, although reduced in many cases, continued. But it was small potatoes compared with the big speculation right here in the United States—in loans and investments. Take mortgages, for example. I don't mean the loans to newlyweds for the purchase of a two-bedroom, suburban layout. I am referring to mortgages on condo-miniums, hotels, office skyscrapers, and supershopping complexes. Then there was the explosive boom in consumer credit and credit cards, which had no precedent. Perhaps, if it had been the fifties and the early sixties, before the days of the big housing boom/bust and before the rampant inflation, big investments in mortgages couldn't be called "speculation." Perhaps if it had been speculation by a Wall Street money manager juggling stocks for some pension fund, it would have been no surprise. But these were banks, not money managers or petty loan sharks. And they were dealing with people's life savings, not go-for-broke investment schemes.

Stockholders First, Depositors Second

Why did the bankers embark on these policies of borrow short and lend long? Why did they begin to fool around with all sorts of money-raising gimmicks and lending schemes just to make a quick buck? If we could somehow get the experience of a banker who was around in those days, he'd probably describe the scene somewhat like this:

The time is early 1961, the place, a commercial bank in Philadelphia. Two junior bank officers march into the office of one of their older colleagues for what appears to be a routine talk on loans. However, there is something unusual in their behavior that puts the older banker on the defensive. "Have you seen our earnings for this quarter?" asks one of the young men.

"Yup!" replies the older man. "Three percent better than 1960. Pretty good, huh?"

"Good? How can you say this is good? Look what the s & l across the street is doing! Don't you realize they've been making at least twice as much as we have? Damn upstarts!"

"Well, uhm, I think—"

"That's right," chimes in the other junior officer. "And you know why, don't you? Because when a borrower gets thumbs down from us, he just walks over to the s & l, and they give him the dough, no questions asked. That's why! They've got the guts to do it. Why can't we have the same kind of guts?"

The older man leans forward over his desk and is about to lecture them about the importance of safety over earnings when the phone rings and his thoughts are frozen in midair. It's the bank's president.

"Just spoke to one of our largest stockholders," he says.

"What about?"

"The man is madder than hell. Says we'd better wake up before it's too late. Says we're letting the banking business slip right through our fingers. That you guys had better get on the ball and make those loans."

"But—but what about the depositors?"

"What about them? When was the last time a depositor asked you what you were doing with his money?"

It was true. The depositors hardly ever paid attention to bank balance sheets, whereas stockholders watched bank earnings carefully. The president hung up, and the two men left. But despite the pressures from above and from below, the older loan officer continued to pursue his own policy of turning down risky loans. Three months later he found himself falling behind his colleagues in promotions. Three years later he could be found near a creek behind a mountain cabin in Canada, fishing for trout. And it wasn't until *two decades* later, when bank stocks began to sink anyhow, that some bankers, according to *Business Week's* September 21, 1974, issue, finally raised their voices against the fact that the "obsession of bank management with earnings growth isn't particularly helpful for depositors."

The Marriage Between the Corporations and Banks

It wasn't enough to make ordinary loans. Banks stuck their necks out and promised their corporate customers that they would have money waiting for them whenever they needed it. These became known as revolving credit agreements, or standby credits. Everybody in the business knew about these future commitments, but nobody knew exactly how much. At one time the Federal Reserve ran a study on standby credit. At first, the Fed was apparently so surprised by its findings that it dared not make them public lest they upset the confidence of savers and investors. Later it was revealed that for every dollar of current loans outstanding there was more or less one dollar of promised future loans. One analyst put it this way: "The banks have kissed nearly every girl in town. What are they going to do if all of them decide they want to go to bed on the same night?"

The union between the banks and the corporations was no mixed marriage. By the time the final vows and promises were made, virtually all the big banks had already converted into full-fledged corporate entities known as bank holding companies. These companies had nearly all the rights and privileges of any business corporation to maneuver with money. They issued bonds and commercial paper. Their stocks were usually traded on the New York Stock Exchange and other leading marketplaces. And, like any corporation, they could borrow from other banks. Most important, these corporations retained outright ownership of DC-10s and 747s, nuclear power plants, and fuel-producing factories. What did the banks do with these properties? They leased them—to businesses.

Because this leasing is off-balance-sheet financing, no one knows just how much of it banks have done, but clearly the amount is in the billions. Much of the nation's fleet of big jet aircraft is leased from banks, and if the financial problems of a large airline get out of hand, some banks could find themselves the perplexed possessors of 747s for which there is often no market.

In 1980 a growing number of banks across the country went one step further—large-scale leasing of automobiles to the average consumer. They reasoned, as reported by the *Wall Street Journal,* that "the increasingly popular five-year loans are risky enough... but if the loans are extended to six or seven years to stay within borrowers' monthly budgets, they become ridiculous, because the car never lasts that long." The banks decided to buy the car themselves, lease it to the customer, and, in the end, wind up taking even more risks.

Big Losses

Thus the white-haired boys who made profits were said to be investing and "hedging," while the poor blokes who took losses (like the trader in Franklin National and the former head of First Pennsylvania) were said to have been "speculating"—the only difference being that some investors were lucky and the others were not. I wondered what would happen if we applied this same definition of the terms "investment" and "speculation" to some of the other goodies the banks had piled up in their portfolios. I picked up the Federal Reserve Bulletin of May 1980 and made these comments: (Bear in mind that at that time bond prices were at their best levels of the year.)

"Let's see now. 'Reporting Member Banks.' That's the big city banks representing about three-quarters of the assets of all commercial banks. Take investments first. What's the first item?

"Oh, U.S. securities due within one year. They've got $6.8 billion, not much loss there—maybe 2 percent, or $136 million. If interest rates go up sharply, it might be more than that, but let's be conservative—give 'em the benefit of the doubt.

"Next, Treasury securities within five years. They've got $18.1 billion. Most likely paid $1,000 for each of those notes and bonds, and now they're selling at about $950, a 3 percent paper loss, or $543 million.

"Then those over five years. There are $5 billion. Must have a paper loss of nearly 10 percent, or at least $450 million.

"Okay. What else have they got? One year or less, $6.8 billion in the portfolio. How much have they gone down? Two percent maybe, that is, $130 million losses.

"How much in total losses does that make so far? About $1,259 million. Not too bad. What's next? 'All other municipal tax-exempt bonds,' it says. Uh-oh! That's the long-term stuff. They've got $45 billion. How in the world did they get stuck with that much? Some of it is off 20 percent, but let's take an average, say, 15 percent. *That's a $6¾ billion paper loss!*

"Still some more. Here it says, 'other bonds, corporate stocks and securities.' Wonder what that really means? Probably IBM, Eastman Kodak, federal agency bonds, some triple A bonds—some bad, some good, but mostly vulnerable. Total is $2.6 billion. With a potentially sick stock and bond market, gotta lop off at least 15 percent for that one, say, $390 million in paper losses. Which leaves a sum total of $8,399 million, $8 billion rounded off. Very, very bad. That's the 'weekly reporting banks.' If you include *all* commercial banks, it would come to about $10 billion.

"Wonder how much the reporting member banks have got in the account called 'reserves for losses on securities'? Maybe they've got enough to cover the losses? Let's see, it's $5,444 *million.* Nope, not enough."

But that was only the stock and bond portfolio. It did not include the *loans.* I estimated paper losses on loans were probably close to $35 to $40 billion for all commercial banks, calculating about a 5 percent decline from book value. Then there were items like passenger cars, customer goods, mobile homes, which are even more vulnerable. This thing is bigger than any Federal Reserve or Federal Deposit Insurance Company. It's bigger than all of them put together.

The above calculations were made when bond prices had reached what I considered to be a temporary peak. In the fictional third section of this book you will see how I expect bond prices will break below the lows of February and March 1980, producing losses that are much more severe.

The "Thrifts"

If you're shocked by what happens to your money in a commercial bank, you had better brace yourself for the bad news on the typical dollar in the average savings and loan association. In 1967 ninety-eight cents of that deposit went into mortgage loans. So to make things simple and easy to understand, I tentatively reasoned that for every dollar deposited two cents were left in cash reserves. *But then, in 1980, the amount of mortgages exceeded the amount in savings.* I realized that I had been oversimplifying. As of the end of March 1980 the s & l's had approximately $478 billion in savings capital. Yet somehow or other they managed to squeeze out approximately $479 billion in mortgage loans. This meant that for every dollar of deposits *over* a dollar was loaned out. How could that be?

Here's how the money and the numbers were juggled. The s & ls had borrowed $43 billion from the Federal Home Loan Bank as compared with only $4 billion in early 1968. At the same time s & l

borrowings from other institutions—commercial banks, etc.—
were $13 billion as compared with only $5 billion in 1968. This
means that the savings and loans had accumulated total debts of
almost $56 billion.

Most of this money was being set aside for cash reserves, freeing
the savings plus a bit extra for mortgages. When you subtract their
borrowings from "cash assets" and "other investment securities,"
you find that the s & l's were left with a deficit of $4 billion in
reserves, or a minus of one cent in reserves for every dollar of
savings deposits. Much of it was in federal agency securities, state
and local government securities, and "miscellaneous securities."
Never in the history of this country was so much backed by so
little.

7

The
Debt Monster

AFTER THIRTY ODD YEARS of unrestrained borrowing by manufacturers, utilities, retailers, banks, and governments, a great debt monster had grown in our midst—an accumulation of $4.4 *trillion* in bonds, mortgages, and loans that threatened to sabotage nearly every economic policy of the Government. As of March 31, 1980, a $1.5 trillion monster roamed the headquarters of our nation's corporations; a $949 billion monster stalked the halls of the Federal Government; and by far the greatest debt monster could be found sitting on the rooftops of nearly every home, office building, and shopping center in America—$1,362 billion in mortgages!

If the debt monster had grown at the same pace as the rest of the economy, there would have been no problem. But this was not the case. Between 1960 and 1979 new debts created every year grew over eleven times, whereas GNP grew by less than five times. The economy was running into the law of diminishing returns—more debts, less results.

If the growth in stock equities—the basic mechanism of our

economic system—had kept pace with the growth in debts, the problem would not have been so severe. But this too was clearly not the case. In 1968 the total market value of all common and preferred stocks in the U.S. was approximately equivalent to the total amount of debts ($1.03 trillion vs. $1.37 trillion). By 1980, however, *debts outnumbered stocks by three and a half to one.*

Had there been sufficient liquid reserves to back up these debts, no problem would have arisen. But no! By 1980 the cash liquidity of corporations, banks, consumers, and governments was *at the lowest point for the twentieth century.*

If the average time span of the debts had been stretched out to the distant future as much as possible, the debtors would at least have had some time in which to "come up with the dough." In fact, debt had become a lighted fuse burning closer and closer to the crisis threshold: In the early 1960s the average time span on the

TABLE 5
Estimated Short-Term Debts in U.S. As of June 1980

	Billions of dollars	
SHORT-TERM MONEY MARKETS		
U.S. Treasury Bills	195	
Commercial Paper	124	
Bank Acceptances	52	
Fed Funds & Other Borrowings	90	
TOTAL		461
NOTES & BONDS COMING DUE WITHIN 12 MOS.		
Treasury Notes & Bonds	40	
Government Agency Bonds	25	
Corporate Bonds & Notes	30	
Municipal Bonds & Notes	20	
TOTAL		115
OTHER CREDIT COMING DUE		
Banks & Trust Loans to Business	116	
Mortgages & Interest	160	
Consumer Credit	240	
TOTAL		516
GRAND TOTAL		1,092

Data: Federal Reserve

Government's debt was five years, but by 1979 it had shortened to three and a half years. Also, in the early 1970s corporations had four times more long-term debts than short-term debts; but by 1979 this ratio had plunged to 2.6 times.

Short-term debts would be the number one driving force behind the Great Money Panic. They were equally the number one blind spot of most American economists. Few realized that debts were coming due virtually at the speed of light—33 thousand dollars per second, $2.7 billion a day, $88 billion a month. *Few understood that, as of June 30, 1980, there was an estimated $1,092 billion in short-term debts. Even if every share of common stock listed on the New York Stock Exchange were sold for cash, it still would not have been enough to pay up the debts coming due within twelve months.*

The debt monster was so appalling to most economists that many often tried to make believe it didn't exist. Some would explain that "for every liability in the balance sheet of one economic entity there is an equivalent asset created in the balance sheet of another," and therefore "the system is in constant equilibrium." What they were really saying is that all balance sheets balance. They forgot that modern accounting was a man-made device *designed* to balance.

Others insisted that "cash-money is lent to A, who in turn lends it to B, C, and D—ad infinitum—stretching in an unlimited chain of credit." They didn't realize that any attempts by the Federal Reserve to print more money resulted in a bond-market collapse and hence less credit—measured in current market-value terms. An explanation made by one of Wall Street's foremost experts on interest rates was no less impractical: "Short-term debts," he told me after a conference in May 1980, "are short term in name only. In reality, they are permanent fixtures of the economy which are naturally refinanced as they come due."

"This might be the case in an expanding economy," I responded, "but what will happen if the economy begins to contract rapidly? How will these debts be refinanced if national income takes a nose dive?"

"Inflation takes care of that" he said with a note of finality.

"Because of inflation the real value of debts outstanding diminishes over time, making them easier and easier to finance." Three months later the truth came out: Real GNP plunged 9.2 percent. Yes, inflation was indeed diminishing the real value of debts outstanding. The problem was that the *ability to pay these debts was declining even faster.*

With these rationalizations economists often managed to hide the debt monster from the public and from themselves. But they were not able to ignore one of the consequences of its rapid growth—inflation.

Inflation was said to be "the most vexing and most intractable of all economic problems," "immovable," "hard to cure." Yet few seemed to know that it was really the debt monster in disguise; that excess credit pumped into the economy stimulated growth in the demand for goods and services at a faster clip than improvements in productivity. Credit wasn't the only cause of inflation, but it was certainly the most consistent cause.

Nevertheless, laymen viewed inflation as a plague that spread from country to country, slowly destroying the society of each. Others saw it as a conspiracy by the rich to bleed the poor, by labor to bleed the rich, or by the politicians to collect votes from *both* the rich *and* the poor. Some economists went no further than the statement that inflation is "too much money chasing too few goods," which, unfortunately, was not an explanation, only a description. Still others dwelled upon the different kinds of inflation: "creeping inflation," "rampant inflation," "runaway inflation," "galloping inflation," "hyperinflation," "cost-push inflation," "demand-pull inflation," "structural inflation," "inflation-fed inflation." Despite the plethora of terms, inflation still defied solution; and repeated plans by Government economists over the years to deal with its causes never got off the ground.

In the early 1970s two schools of thought emerged. One group insisted that the causes of inflation were "structural," meaning, in the jargon of the time, that *labor* was primarily to blame. They said it was due "to the rise of Government unions, the shift of power from union leaders to a more militant rank and file, and a cluster of trends that made strikes more tolerable for labor." The other group of economists proposed a theory that stated in effect: "Inflation causes inflation." They believed that all that was needed was a "one-time push" to bring inflation down.

In an attempt to resolve the debate the Council of Economic Advisors (CEA) undertook a massive study to find the "real causes" of inflation. Responsibility for its progress was turned over by its chairman, Herbert Stein, to Ezra Solomon, who several months later passed the buck to an economist newly arrived at the CEA, Nicholas Perna. In October 1972 Stein appeared before the Joint Economic Committee and was asked by Senator William Proxmire about the status of the study. "We are not prepared to make the conclusions of that study today," Stein said. "We will have more to say about it in our report." But the report, when it finally appeared, made no mention of the study. (*Fortune* for January 1974 discusses this aspect of the subject.) The government economists apparently knew all along that they were pumping too much credit into the economy and feeding the fires of inflation. Their *real* concern was how to prevent a recession and cover up the fact that inflation was the probable consequence of that policy.

One of the few political pressure groups that ever succeeded in temporarily holding back the inflationary tide was the Sound Dollar Committee. This committee organized a mass public campaign, which was to a large degree responsible for the balanced budget of 1960, and later lobbied for restraint in debt creation. In 1970 I decided to call the founder to get his views on the latest betrayal of his philosophy of moderation.

"There's no telling what will happen now," were his first words. "A strong combination of businessmen, bankers, and Wall Street investment bankers is behind the Government all the way. All they care about is keeping the boom alive. So they're throwing all the nation's resources into the pot. They can't help losing control of inflation, credit, foreign and domestic affairs—the works. Sooner or later it'll end up in a big bust—probably a panic."

I decided to play the Devil's advocate to get his reaction. "Can't they prevent that?" I asked. "I mean, look, after all, this is a new system, a modern system. It's not like the twenties and thirties when government and business were powerless to control events.

Now they have all sorts of controls, tools, weapons, barometers, automatic mechanisms."

"Those gimmicks don't prevent a thing," he answered. "They merely prolong the boom and postpone the day of reckoning. The economy is sick, and they're just cramming more of the credit drug down our throats. The only real way to prevent it is to make it happen sooner. Sounds kind of contradictory, doesn't it? But it's a fact. Then you would have *controlled* deflation, instead of *panic* deflation—deliberate, rational, cushioned contraction instead of sudden, chaotic, destructive contraction. The Government would be, say, six months *ahead* of events, not six months behind."

"Sounds good in theory but—"

"But they'll never do it. I know. It's politically unacceptable to say the least."

"That's the understatement of the year," I exclaimed, still playing the Devil's advocate. "Do you realize what that kind of deflationary policy would lead to? It would lead to bankruptcies, massive unemployment, food shortages, maybe even—"

"I know what you're thinking," he said. "You're thinking I'm one of those who believes in the 'survival of the fittest' and 'let the weak suffer.' You think I'm the type who would just sit back and hope for a nice entertaining calamity. But you're forgetting several things. You're forgetting about the material economic forces that no government has yet learned to control. You're forgetting about the limits of the world's supply of resources—and the demand for them. If they continue to expand now, these forces will take over, and the White House will be tossed around like a cardboard shack in a tornado. But if they contract, sure, it'll be tough, but at least they'll be able to steer the events. They'll be able to avoid the big bumps."

"What about the debt monster?" I retorted.

"That's where my bond plan comes in."

"Your bond plan?"

"There are still pockets of liquidity around the country. There are still people who have liquid savings and who haven't thrown themselves into the fire. But they are going fast. Some people who own resources like CDs or municipal bonds think they're safe, but they're really not. What worries me is that by the time the chickens have come home to roost, everything will be locked up in brick and mortar, in TV sets and automobiles, in receiverships and bankruptcy courts. What bothers me is that there may be few liquid resources left for a quick recovery, no easy way for the country to recuperate after the crisis."

"A recovery?" Here it was many years before the bust, and this man was already thinking in terms of recovery.

"Sure. You don't want to see the country go through one of those long, agonizing depressions, do you? You don't want to see breadlines and shantytowns, do you? You want to see a quick, strong comeback, right? What we're doing is building up liquid reserves. Since 1960 we've had a money fund that is invested 100 percent in short-term Treasury bills, only it's going too slowly. Too many people would rather make capital gains than earn a solid income. So we began to think about a way that would attract them and at the same time accomplish the goal of building support for a recovery. That's when I got the idea of the Government bond plan, a totally new concept. People put their liquid reserves into safe Treasury bills, and then later we'll shift them into Government bonds and notes for a possible capital gain."

"Why Government bonds?" I asked.

"They're the centerpiece of the big debt markets. If there's going to be a comeback, it's going to have to start in the Government-security market. The Government-security market is the heart of the debt markets."

"Why the debt markets?"

"The debt markets are the core of all financial markets."

"Most people think it's the stock market."

"It was; it was. But that was in the twenties and thirties. Not now. Now it's the debt markets. It's got at least ten to fifteen times more volume than the stock market."

"Ten to fifteen times?"

"That's right. Ten to fifteen times. You mentioned the debt monster, right? Well, where do you think it will show up first? In the debt markets, the credit markets, the money markets. Whatever you call it, it's the same place, the place where nearly every borrower in the country must go for his credit. If there's going to be another 1929, if there's going to be a credit collapse, it's going to begin in the debt markets, not the stock market."

"So how does your plan work?"

"It works like this. The customer puts up $10,000 and we borrow $90,000 from a bank to make a total of $100,000. We take the $100,000 and buy ninety-day Treasury bills. When interest rates go up sharply, it means that prices for bonds will go *down* sharply. Then, when the prices of Government bonds and notes reach bottom, we buy them and help stimulate a recovery. Our firm gets a commission, the investor gets a capital gain, and maybe, if we can get enough people together, the country will get support when it needs it the most."

"But how can you expect to support the whole bond market?" I asked.

"I figure, at the rate we're going now, we'll control about $1/2 billion in Treasury bills directly and another $10 billion indirectly. If a $1,000 face-value government bond goes to, say, $450 or $550, then we can buy about twice as much worth. Now the government bond market has an average daily volume of about $50 million a day, and I think it could be much less than that when investors lose interest during a panic. So we could have about ten days of buying power directly and much more indirectly."

Ten years later, in early 1980, when the anticipated bond-market collapse finally came, such a plan would have been of great benefit to the nation. Unfortunately, other, more powerful forces had taken over the bond markets.

8

Attempts to Stop
the Panic

IN THE FIRST SEVERAL months of the Nixon Administration
plans were made to tighten up the economy and deflate. But Nixon
knew very little about the dangerous debt monster, let alone that as
much as 20 percent of it was short-term, a literal "time bomb" that
threatened to start ticking away as soon as a recession slowed down
the flow of funds constantly needed to repay these debts.

Interest rates soared. Penn Central, Chrysler, Ling Temco
Vought, and other weak links in the economy were caught unpre-
pared. The stock market broke to 627 on the Dow in May 1970,
and the brokers were going broke. Nixon was terrified of fulfilling
a prediction made by Eisenhower that he would fight inflation but
wind up being killed politically. He decided instead to fight
recession, fight it as no other President in American history ever
had; and Arthur Burns, the new Federal Reserve chairman, coop-
erated fully. The companies that couldn't borrow money in the
collapsing commercial paper market went to their banks. The
banks went to the Fed, and the Fed dished out the money. In his

book *Supermoney*, Adam Smith writes of that fight:

> Some of the bankers who had stayed awake that summer, fretting that if anybody added up the losses in their bond portfolios they might think the bank was busted, were stunned to find that they were having a very good year. Not only had there not been crisis, but the money had been recycled...and everybody lived happily ever after.

Around this time the domestic economy sprang a leak, and the world monetary crisis made its first major appearance. Nixon reacted with a series of economic bombshells. On August 15, 1971, he imposed a ninety-day wage-and-price freeze. He declared a 10 percent surcharge on most imports. Most important, by taking the United States off the gold standard and effectively devaluating the dollar, Nixon dismantled the postwar economic structure based upon the Bretton Woods Agreement of 1944. There are no clear-cut boundaries that separate the boom from the bust, no foolproof ways of determining when the era of postwar growth ended and the era of international stagflation began. However, if someone wanted to select one single event that best symbolized this momentous transition in the economic history of the twentieth century, it might be August 15, 1971.

The growth rate in worker productivity, which had been increasing with only minor interruptions for nearly two hundred years, had begun to slow down—a prelude to actual declines that would begin toward the end of the decade. Later it would be called "the most basic sickness of the American economy." But at the time few made much of the change. The money-and-credit printing presses continued to run at a feverish pitch, propelling the economy toward an encounter with the world's limited supplies of resources and setting the stage for the Arab oil embargo of 1973.

The inflation problem—long a sideshow in the play for economic and political power—burst onto the main arena of American life with gale force. Interest rates soared. Money markets were thrown into chaos. Franklin National and the West German Herstadt Bank went under, and New York City teetered on the brink of collapse. Again the debt monster was unleashed, only bigger and fiercer than ever before. And again the Federal Reserve came to the rescue.

In theory the Federal Reserve was controlling the *supply* of money being pumped into the economy. In practice it was later discovered that they were seeking to control the *cost* of money—interest rates. There was one problem in this strategy. By this time the *net cash assets of corporations were down to a minus $326 billion* versus a *plus* $47 billion in 1955. (They had $75 billion in cash assets versus $401 billion in current liabilities, leaving a net cash deficit of $326 billion.) Banks, governments, and consumers were in the same boat. This in turn gave rise to a chronic shortage of money in the marketplace and a natural, often explosive tendency for interest rates to move up. Therefore, *in order to keep interest rates down, the Fed had to increase the money supply at a much faster pace than was theoretically desirable. The rapid growth in the money supply then fueled more speculation, more demand for funds, more inflation, and finally even lower liquidity ratios.*

The Federal Reserve governors were not fully aware of the importance of this chronic liquidity shortage in the economy. But they were painfully familiar with its consequences. They discovered that whenever they tried to hold back money-supply growth for too long, an instant credit crunch popped out of nowhere. Thus it was with a sense of moral obligation and patriotic duty that they deliberately went about their business of pumping up the money supply in an attempt to hold interest rates down artificially.

The usual mechanism was quite simple. They handed the money over to New York bond dealers in exchange for government securities. The dealers immediately deposited these funds into their checking accounts at the commercial banks. This extra cash in the banking system then reduced the federal funds rate—the rate at which banks borrowed from each other. Finally all interest rates declined.

Regarding the question of what was happening behind the scenes, very few know the answer. However, in the August 1977 issue of my monthly publication, *Money & Markets,* I ventured to guess. The remainder of this chapter is a condensed version of that issue. Please bear in mind that, although all the facts and figures are based on actual Federal Reserve statistics, the dialogues are primarily the product of my own imagination. *Also, note the unusually close resemblance of the problems confronting the Fed in 1975 with those of 1980.*

The Great Bond Pool

The time is April 14, 1975. The place is the Federal Reserve Building, Constitution Avenue, Washington, D.C. Eleven members of the Federal Reserve Open Market Committee sit at a long conference table. Chairman [Arthur] Burns opens the meeting.

"Only eight months ago," he says, "money markets were on the verge of a full-scale collapse. We managed to ease credit dramatically, and we have breathed a sigh of relief for the moment. But only for a moment. Three weeks from today the Treasury Department will hit the bond market with the most massive financing week on record—a $3.8 billion refunding operation plus another $2 billion to be raised in net new cash. Senator Humphrey has been on my tail trying to find out what we intend to do about it; so I wrote him a letter to the effect that it's too unpredictable; that there is no way of estimating the impact of this thing. He is right about one thing, though. We may not be doing enough to soften its potential impact on money markets."

The man at the far side of the conference table is perplexed. "What more can we do? In the past thirty days, we've pumped over $7 billion, mostly in the outright net purchases of government securities. Seven billion dollars! That's already a flagrant violation of our own guidelines."

"What guidelines?" asks one of the newer members. "I thought the Fed-funds target rate was our primary concern."

"Back in March 1972 we informally agreed that about $2½ billion should be our limit for any given month. Since that time we've surpassed the limit only once—in August 1974, when we bought a record of $3.3 billion to prevent interest rates from running away. And we thought that was a lot!" he adds with sarcasm. "Now we've pumped over twice our previous record in order to support bond prices and hold interest rates down. And what good has it done? We did manage to prevent three-month T-bill rates from hitting 6 percent last week, but the longer-term bonds are still sinking. I honestly think there is nothing more we can do."

A prolonged silence descends on the conference room. Each man scans his own mind for alternative solutions to the dilemma, realizing, however, that there is really only one way out. Finally, a fourth member puts it into words. "Buy more! Buy more bonds. Hold those interest rates down!"

The chairman makes no effort to hide his growing impatience. "How? Where? You heard the man. We have already gone way out on a limb. We have to maintain some semblance of a balance in the money supply, don't we?"

"Not if it means letting Fed funds hit 13 percent again. Not if it means killing the incipient recovery! The automobile and housing industries were hurt badly by the last round of tight money, and their wounds have yet to heal."

"We're at a very touchy point in the cycle," chimes in another member. "Real output declined in March, but at a slower pace, implying that a turnaround may be in the making and that a recovery could get under way by the third quarter. But unemployment is up from 8.2 to 8.7 percent; auto sales fell as soon as the price rebates were discontinued; and perhaps most dangerous of all, the tax-exempt market is still a shambles. To permit another run-up in interest rates would be tantamount to sabotage. So I say we make an all-out effort to pave the way for the Treasury well ahead of time. I say we buy another $3 or $4 billion before the end of April, while we still have a chance."

A man who normally sides with Burns suddenly turns against him. "You said yourself it's the only tool we've got left. So if $3 or $4 billion is not enough, we must do it again and again until we're over the hump."

And so they did. The unprecedented $7.1 billion in Government securities purchased between March 12 and April 16, 1975, was followed by another $6.2 billion between April 16 and April 30. Within several weeks the Federal Reserve pumped nearly $13.3 billion into the banking system. With purchases for the month of April alone coming to nearly 250 percent more than the previous record made in August 1974, it is little wonder that the Treasury's financing went so smoothly. There arose a new wave of enthusiasm among dealers, and cheers resounded from the back offices of Wall Street to the Oval Office of the White House. They didn't realize that, even as the Fed was saving the day in the spring of 1975, it was giving birth to a money-market monster that could show its teeth several years later.

Two weeks go by, and the scene shifts to the phone-cluttered desk of a major New York dealer in government securities.

"Hey! Do you know how much the Fed bought this week?" whispers a veteran bond trader.

"No, how much?" replies a junior colleague.

"Would you believe it, over $5 billion?"

"You must be joshing!"

"Nope, looks like the Fed's in this thing all the way. They're scared the Treasury's going to bring on another panic, and that's good, because it means they're going to just keep right on buying. Bills, notes, bonds—anything that needs support."

"Then let's get in on the act," exclaims the younger man. "I know our inventories are kind of big, but with the Fed practically guaranteeing easy money, we can't lose. Let's load up on anything we can lay our hands on."

The veteran trader isn't quite as enthusiastic. There's something in the tone of this brief exchange that brings back echoes of a similar conversation he overheard as a young boy nearly fifty years ago: "Hey! You know who's buying?" said the voice. "Raskob. That's who. He's going to run up the price till kingdom come—our chance to make a killing, a big killing."

That was 1929. The Dow Jones was going great guns, and the stock pools were still hot. In those days he was an errand boy at Ungerleider and Company. Now he is senior vice-president in the government securities division of one of the top investment banking houses. He is beginning to wonder whether these flashbacks are some kind of subconscious warning signal or merely random associations when the other dealer breaks into his thoughts with those same familiar words: "This is our chance to make a killing, a big killing."

There are striking similarities between the stock pools of the late twenties and what I call the Great Bond Pool of the late seventies. The graphs on page 76 will illustrate why. They are especially designed to let you see at a glance the three main arenas in this unfolding drama: The actions of the Federal Reserve (top), the movement of interest rates (middle) and the behavior of bond owners or traders (bottom).

In the top graph note how the Fed's purchases of April 1975 stick out like a sore thumb (month marked with arrow). As you can see in the middle graph, because of the big injection of funds, interest rates did not go up very much despite the fact that the Treasury sold record amounts of new issues. This is what the Federal Reserve had hoped and expected. What they did not expect is the effect of their actions on the bottom graph.

For over a quarter of a century the volume of trading in United States Government securities had increased at a gradual and stable rate of 26 percent per year. Then, as a direct consequence of the Fed's continued support, the bond market went wild with activity. The growth rate soared to 221 percent, and within twenty-eight months average daily volume mushroomed from $2½ billion to $15 billion. *The equivalent of five new bond markets was created virtually overnight.*

There is nothing wrong with big volume. The problem is that the bulk of the big buying came only *after* interest rates fell most of the way, only at a time when bond prices were approaching their peaks. You can see this clearly in the graphs if you compare stage 1 and stage 2 of the interest-rate decline (the bond-market rally). The implication is that the bulk of investors were suckered in at low rates and high prices. Investors were lured by the aura of safety, assured by the continued promises of support by the Government and finally won over by a new style of aggressive promotion techniques. Bache used its relatively recent Halsey Stuart acquisition to enlarge further its government-bond division.

12. THE GREAT BOND POOL

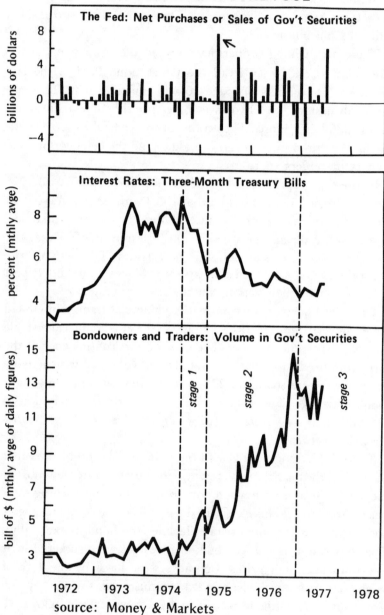

source: Money & Markets

Other big houses, among them Lehman Brothers and Paine Webber, alerted their account executives to push all kinds of bonds. Smaller regional houses found that their relatively conservative customers were natural buyers. Virtually the entire investment community joined the bond-market bandwagon. Soon the fever spread to government agency bonds, local revenue bonds, all varieties of mortgage bonds. And still you could hear the same words echoing around the country: "You know who's behind this thing? The Federal Reserve, that's who!"

As in 1929, a handful of large buyers led the flock. In those days it was the Durants, the Raskobs, the Mitchells, and the Wigginses. This time it was the Federal Reserve. In both eras investors felt they were protected by an umbrella of security while huge trading volume was generated. Then the big volume was in stocks like radio and GM. This time the big volume has been in the three- to seven-year notes and bonds—securities that enjoy big swings in price but require relatively little in margin. Most important, as in the 1929 stock pools, the majority of the new bond buyers came into the marketplace after the lucky few had chalked up the bulk of the paper profits.

In the final stages of the stock pool of 1929 stockholders were surprised to discover there was little or no support in the marketplace, even at relatively low levels. The hundreds of thousands of new buyers had already committed the bulk of their resources and refused to buy many more, complaining they already had too many paper losses. They were locked in at relatively high prices. When they finally got word that the pool leaders themselves were getting out, they unleashed wave after wave of selling pressure.

The same is bound to happen in bond markets.

9

The Government
Loses Control

THE FEDERAL RESERVE finally withdrew its support for bond
markets in October 1979. Reason: the great dollar collapse. Back in
the early 1970s only a small minority of jeremiahs had expected it.
In retrospect, the sequence of events was now clear: President
Nixon, in his dollar devaluation of August 1971, cut the dollar
loose from its moorings; the Fed's chairman, Arthur Burns, with
his record-shattering pump-priming operation, pushed it out to
unchartered waters; and the new Federal Reserve Chairman, G.
William Miller, was confronted with the impossible task of sailing
across the Atlantic and the Pacific with no compass and no rudder.

"Let's see, now. What went wrong?" comments an official at the
Fed to his assistant. "We pumped the money into the bond
markets, right?"

"Right."

"The bond dealers then deposited it into the banks, right?"

"Right."

"And then the banks lent the money to U.S. corporations; the
U.S. corporations invested the money into plant and equipment;
and the U.S. economy got all the benefit, right?"

"Miller's Dilemma"

Wrong! The overwhelming majority of American billionaire manufacturers—controlling over 60 percent of all assets of manufacturing companies—were multinational corporations, deriving one-third of their earnings from overseas. These multinationals had the option to funnel their investments into those areas where production costs were the lowest and worker productivity the highest—in short, the nation with the lowest inflation. With the U.S. Treasury running back-to-back budget deficits in 1975-76, totaling $101 billion, and with the U.S. Federal Reserve stimulating more credit expansion than ever before, it was only natural that the U.S. inflation rate would be among the highest of the great economic powers.

At the same time, American corporations enjoyed a greater access to credit than their counterparts in Europe and Japan. They established subsidiaries abroad, beat down the foreign competition, and got higher investment returns than they would have gotten in the United States, where the market was often approaching a saturation point. IBM, for instance, noticing that domestic business was falling off in 1969, pushed sales at foreign subsidiaries. Coca-Cola, running into stiff competition from Pepsi-Cola and others, gave top priority to its overseas markets. Du Pont, Kodak, ITT, and, of course, the oil giants were also at the head of the pack.

These multinationals opened dollar accounts at the subsidiaries of American banks in London, Paris, or Frankfurt, and it was these new overseas dollars that became the first "Eurodollars." In 1960 the Eurodollar market was a mere niche in the back offices of European banks, with $500 million on deposit. By 1970 it had grown to $50 *billion;* and, by March 31, 1980, it had ballooned to *$820* billion!

Analysts often wondered why the Eurodollar market grew so fast. One important reason was the credit creation in the United States. The pace of new credit created every year in the U.S. is closely correlated to the net increases in Eurodollars and the companion "Eurocurrencies" abroad. Despite many other crosscurrents, this is the picture that emerges: the U.S. Federal Reserve pumped the money, and the money escaped overseas.

The Eurodollar market was dangerous for several reasons. First, it often functioned like an offshore casino—a no-man's-land in which multinational giants, wealthy individuals, and major world governments bid for deposits and speculated for quick profits; a free-for-all unregulated by central banks, unrestrained by cash-reserve requirements, and uninsured by any public or private body. It was also a key vehicle used by international banking consortia to take in short-term deposits from oil-producing nations and make long-term loans to the financially fragile less developed countries.

The most immediate danger was the fact that, unlike the average American saver, the Eurodollar owners were, oftener than not, willing to sell these dollars in exchange for another currency whenever they thought they might be able to get a higher interest rate, or whenever the other currency seemed less threatened by inflation, balance of payments deficits, or political crisis.

This presented the Fed's William Miller with a Catch-22 dilemma: If he continued the policy of holding down U.S. interest rates despite accelerating inflation, international investors would dump the dollars in massive amounts, causing the value of the dollar to collapse. On the other hand, if he let interest rates rise, the savings and loan industry would suffer massive withdrawals, and the housing industry would collapse. His choices, therefore, were clear: either fly outward in the wildest psychedelic trip of the century or collapse inward with the risk of a depression and the certainty of defeat for the President in the 1980 election; that is, rampant inflation or rampant deflation. Either burst or bust.

He chose the former. Between early 1977 and late 1978—within a matter of twenty-four short months—the dollar plunged from nearly 300 to 175 against the yen, from 2.4 to 1.8 versus the West German mark, and from 2.5 to 1.5 vis-à-vis the Swiss franc. It was the sharpest drop in American currency since the collapse of the Continental money in the late 1770s.

Finally, by the fall of 1979 key OPEC countries, wary of receiving payment for their oil in progressively cheaper dollars, were threatening to shift from the dollar to a basket of currencies —a move that well-regarded money experts predicted would surely destroy the financial structure of the world. The following diary illustrates the sequence of events that ensued.

Belgrade, October 1, 1979. The newly appointed Federal Reserve chairman, Paul Volcker, has flown here to the annual convention of the International Monetary Fund and is coming under intense pressure from West European central banks to take swift action to protect the dollar. Some at the convention are painting the scenario of a new dollar collapse that will make the 1977-78 debacle look like child's play.

Washington, October 6, 1979. After a sudden departure from the IMF meeting on Tuesday and after round-the-clock meetings with Administration officials on Thursday and Friday, Chairman Volcker has just announced "a Draconian bombshell"—a 2 percent hike in the discount rate, stiffer controls on Eurodollar borrowings by U.S. banks, and a drastic shift of emphasis from the manipulation of interest rates to more direct control over bank reserves.

New York City, October 11, 1979. More than three years (and two successive Federal Reserve chairmen) after its creation by Burns, the overgrown bond-market monster is here. Prices on thirty-year Government bonds have plunged by four points in merely four days: and the $1-billion IBM issue—hailed only weeks ago as a brilliant piece of corporate finance—is being described by a consensus of Wall Street analysts as "the greatest underwriting fiasco of all time."

Teheran, November 4, 1979. Iranian students have taken over the U.S. Embassy. Fears of another oil crunch are sweeping the globe.

Kabul, Christmas 1979. The Soviets have invaded Afghanistan.

New York, January 1980. Talk of "a new cold war economy," plus a month-to-month consumer price inflation at an annual rate of some 18 percent, is sending bond markets into a nose dive. Will it be as bad as the October collapse of last year?

New York, February 5, 1980. Yields on longest-term U.S. Government securities have just broken through the 11 percent level—the all-time peak reached during the Civil War. "Faced with a prolonged buyers' strike," exclaims one professional trader quoted in the *Wall Street Journal*, "we decided to throw in the towel and get yields up to a level where some cash buyers might be shocked off the sidelines. We have never had psychology this bearish without some particular incident."

Most experts are saying that the Afghanistan invasion and the resulting inflationary fears are the main causes of the collapse. "Why should investors buy bonds yielding 12 or even 13 percent if they expect inflation is going to be running at 18 or 20 percent?" they explain. This makes sense, but it's only the surface. What they don't understand is that the main cause of inflation is the debt monster; and that the reason the collapse in bonds is so severe is because of the Great Bond Pool now completely abandoned by the pool leader—the Federal Reserve. Buyers lured in at much higher levels are now looking for any excuse to get out, and inflation is the most obvious one.

New York, February 6, 1980. Some panicky holders of bonds are willing to unload at almost any price, but there are few takers. According to the *Wall Street Journal* of February 7, the flood of sell orders prompted all except four or five of the largest, best capitalized bond houses effectively to abandon their "market-making role."

New York, February 11, 1980. The long-term bond market, the core of the financial system of the Western world is, according to dealers, "being pushed perilously close to the point of temporarily ceasing to function." "Forget talking about loss of an 'efficient market.' We lost that weeks ago," says one serious observer. The *Wall Street Journal* of February 12 reports that *traders at major institutions yesterday were unable to find buyers for amounts as little as five million dollars of Treasury bonds.*

New York, February 14, 1980. The pressures on the Government to take outright deflationary action are mounting by the minute. If Uncle Sam cannot find enough investors willing to buy his bonds, he will have to close up shop and start a new government. At the same time, by some estimates investors have had losses totaling at least 25 percent of the market value of their bond holdings in recent months, or more than $400 billion. The *Wall Street Journal* quotes a source at one sizable bank in the East who says that, if he had to liquidate his holdings of Treasury notes, the loss would amount to more than $225 million, wiping out the bank's capital.

Look at this *thing* coming off the Dow Jones wires: "Unless those that brought us this disgusting inflation want to see a government, corporate, and tax-exempt market worth $3.1 trillion and a mortgage market worth $1.32 trillion wiped out, it is clear they are going to have to do something such as much tighter monetary and fiscal policy. If that includes taking away the money that has made this sickening inflationary party possible, then we could have an awesome hangover."

New York, February 19, 1980. But the collapse continues to

gather momentum. According to AP-Dow Jones, the bond market is reeling through "an even blacker Tuesday as inflation and interest rate fears send prices lower." Treasury bonds lost about 4 percent of their face value in yesterday's trading, surpassing the drop of about 2.5 percent that had caused traders to refer to February 5 as "black Tuesday."

New York, February 21, 1980. Henry Kaufman of Salomon Brothers, speaking before the American Bankers Association in Los Angeles, has called for the declaration of a national emergency. On Wall Street bond prices were slightly higher until, as described by one dealer, "Henry K. at the A.B.A. in L.A. touched off another steep market slide."

New York, February 24, 1980. Pessimism on Wall Street is reaching a peak. The bond-market collapse is now about *three times worse* than the October collapse. Will our nation survive it? Strangely, few Americans even know it's happening; but according to the latest definition on Wall Street, "a coward is someone who quits the bond business to go fight against Russian troops in Afghanistan." In just one week, as reported in the *Wall Street Journal* on February 25, some tax-exempt bonds plunged as much as 8 points, or $80 for each $1,000 face value, in the "worst debacle recorded."

Despite the pessimism, rumors last week that President Carter would announce a package of credit controls sent prices soaring upward as much as seven points within a matter of minutes, the most rapid price movement in history, only to fall back again when the rumors were denied. Could it be the signal of a big rally to come?

A White House spokesman has appeared before reporters to say that the Administration is considering a new anti-inflation package. But after twenty years of anti-inflation gimmicks that never worked, Wall Street is skeptical. The word is that credit controls, even if announced, probably won't work. *They are completely unaware of the key role that credit has played in pumping up the inflationary boom.*

West Palm Beach, February, 29, 1980. It is my opinion that mounting pressure on Washington will result in some form of credit controls. We expect the following to come out of such an announcement:

1. The strengthening of bond prices as the first phase of a major rally gets under way.
2. A severe drop in the stock market.
3. A substantial drop in the gross volume of sales in retailing, wholesaling and manufacturing businesses.
4. A falloff in the demand for a host of commodities such as meats, grains, fibers, petroleum products, etc.
5. Sharp declines in corporate profits as very high break-even points take their toll in one business after another.
6. Any major slash in new credit creation which started gradually in the fall of 1978 will be ominous for gold and silver as well as a variety of inflation hedges. (Martin D. Weiss Research, Inc., *Flash Release*, West Palm Beach, February 29, 1980)

Washington, March 14, 1980. Carter's credit control package was finally announced today. Chairman Volcker has reluctantly agreed to clamp down on credit cards, impose stiff reserve requirements on nonmember banks, hit all banks with a special 3 percent surcharge, and, in effect, shut off a good many credit valves.

New York, April 4, 1980. Over the past seven weeks bond markets have continued to zigzag in a sideways pattern. Wall Street is still dissappointed with Carter's credit controls package. Salomon Brothers, for example, says that consumer credit—the primary target of the new credit-tightening policies—represents only a small portion of the total credit outstanding, and that automobile credit, which the Carter Administration chose to leave untouched, represents a substantial portion thereof. They imply it will probably not do the trick in slowing down the economy, and they're recommending that customers stay away from long-term bonds.

New York, May 1980. The economy is in a nose dive—the sharpest since the Great Depression—and Wall Street, which only a few weeks ago was worried credit controls were too weak, is already talking about "economic overkill." People can't get credit. So they're not buying. It's that simple.

Brokers and investors, assuming that recession and lower infla-

tion will bring a permanent decline in interest rates, are buying bonds as though they were going out of style; and so bond prices are soaring. It's the biggest rally in history! Even Henry Kaufman of Salomon Brothers, reversing his earlier stand, now says that "the bond market is reborn." They still don't understand the dynamics of the Great Bond Pool; and the fact that either inflation or deflation, whichever comes first, will put strong pressure on investors and creditors to get rid of a large portion of their $4.4 trillion in bonds and loans.

New York, July 1980. The Federal Reserve has dismantled Carter's credit controls, and the economy is showing initial signs of a sharp—but probably short-lived—bounceback. Bond prices are still near the peak of their historic rally, and everything—especially the Dow Jones industrials—looks great. If you have read this far, you will realize, however, that the basic conditions that have caused the crisis remain unresolved; and that these conditions still place your savings, your investments, and your business in jeopardy.

Ideas for protective steps you may take are provided in the following section. I trust they will serve as a guide for financial survival and constructive action in the difficult times ahead.

BOOK
II

A Guide for
Survival
and
Action

"LET'S RUN SOME ERRANDS TO MAKE UP FOR PAST MISTAKES"

10

What to Do with Your Savings

YOU'RE BACK in your bank. The time is 1980. But now you know: Much of the money you deposited is probably being thrown in with hot money invested in sinking tax-exempt bonds, loaned out for a myriad of risky projects, and sometimes used in foreign-currency speculation. So you are tempted to run back to the counter, make out a withdrawal slip, and close out your account. You begin to build a blacklist. Such-and-such a bank, you hear, has got big paper losses in municipal bonds. Another bank, according to a story in last week's *Wall Street Journal,* is heavily loaned out to less developed countries, etc. Then you begin to wonder, "Am I behaving rationally?" You can't write off banks altogether, because that would be unfair to the *safe* banks. On the other hand, you have no way of judging to what degree these problems will spread to the "system" as a whole. You decide to follow three rules of thumb.

Rule No. 1: Avoid Problem Banks

First you take a good look at the balance sheets, then you ask the following questions:

1. How much of your money deposited in the bank is locked up in loans and how much is left in "equity"? See column B of Table 6.

2. In the event that some of these loans or investments turn sour, how much of a cushion does the bank have in capital? Commercial banks have some $800 billion in loans outstanding as of mid-1980, 15 percent of which are potentially questionable. But they have only $85 billion in capital. If the going gets rough and the earnings of their customers begin to disappear, the danger is great that the capital of many commercial banks could be wiped out. Is your bank one of them? Check column C.

3. What is the bank's liquidity? In other words, how much cash and equivalent plus investments—with appropriate "haircuts" to reflect potential losses—does the bank have to cover deposits and other liabilities? See column D.

4. Last, how does one bank compare with another? We rank the banks in accordance to how they stand up to the above three measures. See column E.

These measures do not cover *every* aspect of banking. Consequently, there may be exceptional banks that rank low on the chart but are in relatively good shape. As a whole, however, it is a good way of distinguishing the safe banks from the problem banks. If at all possible, I believe you should do as much of your banking as you can with the top ten.

As of December 31, 1979, Irving Trust Company (Charter New York Corporation) was near the top of the list, number 1 in equity, number 28 in capital, and number 1 in liquidity. Average rank—8. On the other hand, Citibank (Citicorp), despite its great size and power, was near the bottom of the list. Average rank—47.

During the first half of the twentieth century it was precisely the opposite. While Irving Trust struggled to keep its liquidity from falling below 30 percent, the predecessors of Citicorp—National City Bank and First National of New York—were highly liquid

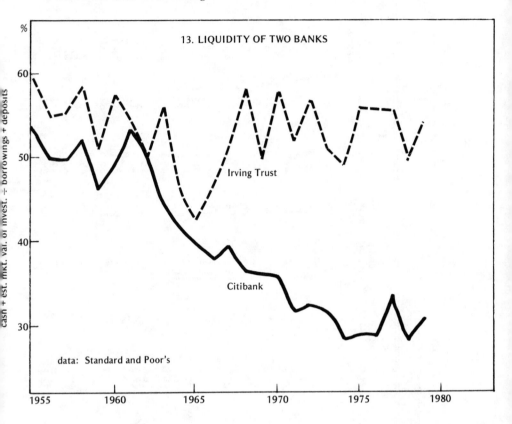

13. LIQUIDITY OF TWO BANKS

cash + est. mkt. val. of invest. ÷ borrowings + deposits

Irving Trust

Citibank

data: Standard and Poor's

and widely respected, maintaining a liquidity ratio above 50 percent for forty-seven out of fifty years. But, beginning in the early fifties, a group of expansionist lawyers and bankers took over and, as illustrated in the accompanying graph, permitted the liquidity to decline to 30 percent. Meanwhile, at Irving Trust the policies of the older generation of bankers, instituted by Lewis Pearson and his colleagues, were strictly maintained. Their liquidity ratio improved and was kept above 50 percent.

Citicorp then became deeply enmeshed in international hot money. It apparently accepted the extremely short-term deposits from oil-producing nations—sometimes for as little as three or four days—and put much of these funds into longer-term loans that ran for months. The oil money was "recycled," but Citicorp continued to accept deposits on these terms and was caught in a

TABLE 6

Which Banks Are the Safest?

A Our Rank		B "Equity" percent	rank	C Capital/Loans percent	rank	D Liquidity percent	rank	E Our Safety Rating
1	Southeast Banking Corp. (Miami)	40.1	3	12.1	9	46.2	8	6.7
2	National City Corp. (Cleveland)	33.1	14	15.2	2	47.5	4	6.7
3	NCNB Corp. (Charlotte)	36.7	7	10.7	14	50.4	2	7.7
4	Nothern Trust Corp. (Chicago)	39.6	5	12.6	7	42.8	12	8.0
5	National Detroit Corp. (Detroit)	34.1	11	13.4	4	44.5	10	8.3
6	First City Bancorp of Tex. (Houston)	40.8	2	10.0	20	46.2	6	9.3
7	Bank of New York Co. (New York)	37.5	6	10.1	17	46.2	7	10.0
8	Charter New York Corp. (New York)	48.8	1	8.4	28	55.5	1	10.0
9	Harris Bankcorp (Chicago)	33.6	12	10.5	15	46.2	5	10.7
10	Citizens & Southern Nat'l Bank (Atlanta)	35.7	8	11.1	13	41.4	15	12.0
11	First Internat'l Bancshares, Inc. (Dallas)	34.2	10	10.1	19	44.0	11	13.3
12	Mellon National Corp. (Pittsburgh)	28.7	23	12.7	6	42.6	13	14.0
13	Texas Commerce Bancshares Inc. (Houston)	37.3	15	10.1	18	40.2	20	14.3
14	Wachovia Corp. (Winston Salem)	30.7	16	12.1	8	40.3	19	14.3
15	Union Bancorp	40.0	4	8.2	32	46.1	9	15.0
16	Detroit Bank Corp. (Detroit)	26.8	26	12.8	5	46.1	18	16.3
17	Pittsburgh National Corp. (Pittsburgh)	27.3	25	11.4	10	41.2	17	17.3
18	Girard Co. (Bala Cynwyd)	25.8	30	14.3	3	39.0	23	18.7
19	Republic of Texas Corp. (Dallas)	30.0	19	9.4	23	42.1	14	18.7
20	BancOhio Corp. (Columbus)	30.7	17	11.2	11	35.5	32	20.0
21	First Nat'l Boston Corp. (Boston)	18.7	40	8.9	25	49.6	3	22.7
22	J.P. Morgan & Co. (New York)	26.1	29	8.7	27	41.4	16	24.0
23	BankAmerica Corp. (San Francisco)	35.0	9	6.2	41	38.2	25	25.0
24	Cleve Trust Corp. (Cleveland)	15.8	43	15.9	1	32.3	34	26.0
25	Manufacturers Hanover Corp. (New York)	33.2	13	6.1	42	38.0	26	27.0

26	First Bank System Inc. (Minneapolis)	24.5	33	10.3	16	33.5	33	27.3
27	First Chicago Corp. (Chicago)	26.3	28	7.7	35	40.1	21	28.0
28	Philadelphia Nat'l Corp. (Philadelphia)	23.3	35	9.9	21	37.8	28	28.0
29	European American BankCorp (New York)	30.1	18	6.5	39	37.7	29	28.7
30	Valley Nat'l Bank of Ariz. (Phoenix)	29.8	20	5.9	43	21.5	49	29.0
31	Mercantile Texas Corp. (Dallas)	21.7	37	9.2	25	38.0	27	29.7
32	Bankers Trust New York Corp. (New York)	28.8	22	5.8	46	39.6	22	30.0
33	Northwest BanCorp (Minneapolis)	22.2	36	9.7	22	31.7	35	31.0
34	Western BanCorp (Los Angeles)	28.8	21	7.3	36	30.7	38	31.7
35	U.S. BanCorp (Portland)	17.4	41	11.1	12	28.6	44	32.3
36	Manufacturers Nat'l Corp. (Detroit)	23.9	34	8.8	26	30.0	41	33.7
37	First Wisconsin Corp. (Milwaukee)	25.3	32	7.3	37	38.8	24	34.0
38	Marine Midland Banks Inc. (Buffalo)	28.0	24	5.3	50	37.1	30	34.7
39	Chemical New York Corp. (New York)	29.8	20	5.9	43	21.5	49	37.3
40	National Bank of North America	14.3	45	9.3	24	30.4	39	38.0
41	Michigan National Corp. (Bloomfields Hill)	21.1	38	8.4	30	25.7	47	38.3
42	Crocker National Corp. (San Francisco)	25.7	31	7.1	38	25.9	46	38.3
43	Sea First Corp. (Seattle)	19.6	39	8.1	33	26.8	45	39.0
44	First Penn Corp. (Philadelphia)	13.9	46	7.7	34	29.5	42	47.7
45	Ranier BanCorp (Seattle)	9.3	49	8.4	31	28.9	43	41.0
46	Chase Manhattan Corp. (New York)	17.1	42	5.7	49	30.7	37	42.7
47	CitiCorp (New York)	11.0	48	5.8	47	31.2	36	43.7
48	Security Pacific Corp. (Los Angeles)	12.5	47	6.5	40	24.5	48	45.0
49	Continental Ill. Corp. (Chicago)	2.7	50	5.8	48	30.3	40	46.0
50	Wells Fargo and Company (San Francisco)	15.4	44	5.9	44	17.8	50	46.0

vise. The biggest gamble was in consumer loans exceeding $13 billion by 1980. But there was a crunching problem. Because Citicorp had to finance them with money that was enormously expensive, and because usury laws typically put ceilings on the rates they could charge, they were stuck with a highly unprofitable business. The result was a 33 percent profit decline in the first quarter of 1980. The problem was further aggravated by the growing frequency of consumer loan defaults in a deepening business recession. With the new easy-to-go-bankrupt law in effect, Washington reported that individuals were taking advantage of it in increasing numbers as personal bankruptcies across the nation soared to record levels.

Rule No. 2: Stick With Twenty-Four-Hour Liquidity

Simply because news of emergency loans to save large corporations, defaults by less developed countries, or investigations of "problem banks" don't make the headlines every day doesn't mean their troubles are over. Even if there is a temporary comeback in business or a money-pumping operation by the Fed, beneath the surface the fundamental situation is not getting better. On the New York Stock Exchange, in foreign-exchange markets, and in nearly all financial capitals of the world you see the extremes of either panic or euphoria, either boom or bust, but little sign of stability and balance. Therefore you should retain—at all times— the flexibility to move in and out within twenty-four hours. Short-term, three-month U.S. Treasury bills meet this requirement because of the highly liquid secondary market where you can sell them, even before maturity if necessary. You pay no interest penalty and there is never more than a very minute loss in principal, if any.

Money funds, you discover, also provide twenty-four-hour liquidity. The Atlantic Fund for Investment in U.S. Government Securities, founded in 1959, was the first of the money funds. (In his book *Eight and One Half Percent and Complete Safety,*

published in New York by Capital Advisors in 1966, J. Irving
Weiss discusses this subject in detail.) It was subsequently taken
over by the Federated group, now one of the largest when
combining the assets of its four money funds—Federated Master
Trust, Trust for Short-Term U.S. Government Securities (for
institutions only), Money Market Management (primarily for
large investors), and Federated Money Market (for all investors).
Later some of the large brokerage firms finally woke up to the idea,
suggested many years earlier by the Atlantic Fund, that they could
hold onto customers who liquidated their portfolios by moving
them into an in-house money fund—a kind of way station where
the money would sit temporarily until new stock and bond positions were taken. Thus we see that the largest money fund today is
Merrill Lynch Ready Assets, with Dean Witter's Intercapital
Liquid Assets Fund, E.F. Hutton's Cash Reserve Management
Fund, and several others not far behind.

However, sheer size should not influence you when shopping
for a money fund. Safety, yield, and average maturity are far more
important (see Table 7). You should be especially concerned with
safety. As long as there is no money panic, there is no immediate
danger for any of the funds listed in the table. The trouble is that
the crisis can come without much advance warning. Therefore, you
don't want to be caught by surprise one day with a fund that owns
securities such as:

1. *Government agency bonds.* Even if short-term, these could
suffer losses in principal and temporarily become entangled in
defaults in the latter stages of the crisis. The Trust for Short-Term
Government Securities, for example, had 89 percent of its assets in
these agency bonds.

2. *Certificates of deposit.* Large withdrawals from banks and
thrift institutions, although temporarily halted by the bank's new
"money market certificates," could resume when the cost of competing directly with the Treasury for funds begins to squeeze bank
profits. Without fresh new CD money coming in, how will the
banks meet old CDs coming due? Apparently, most money funds
haven't thought much about that possibility, because CDs have
been their favorite medium.

TABLE 7

How to Pick the Best Money Funds

As of June 1980	Assets ($ millions)	Current 30 day yield	Avg. maturity (days)	Liquidity (cash and equivalent) as a percent of total assets
Capital Preservation Fund	727.2	10.4	18	100%
Cash Equivalent Fund	914.0	16.1	26	—0—
Cash Reserve Mgt.	2684.3	19.0	71	3.6%
Daily Cash Accum. Fund	2190.9	13.1	39	39.6%
Delaware Cash Res.	506.1	14.8	60	—0—
Dreyfus Liq. Assets	3110.0	15.9	43	1.2%
Federated Money Market Trust	1096.1	13.6	45	3%
Fidelity Daily Income Trust	3039.0	14.0	64	3%
InterCapital Liquid Assets Fund	3735.4	14.9	72	4.2%
Liquid Capital Income	861.3	12.5	22	24.0%
Merrill Lynch Ready Assets	10973.3	17.9	64	20.2%
Money Mart Assets	1709.0	15.7	42	4%
National Liquid Reserves	1431.1	13.8	41	3.4%
Oppenheimer Monetary	605.0	13.1	20	—0—
Paine Webber Cash Fund	2294.7	13.9	36	13%
Reserve Fund	1880.0	13.4	16	19%
Rowe Price Prime Reserve	1083.7	13.7	38	1%
Shearson Daily Dividend	1874.9	13.3	23	—0—
Temp. Fund	2522.8	13.6	36	6%
Webster Cash Reserve	443.4	13.2	38	4%

For most recent figures, see Donaghue's Money Fund Reports, Holliston, Mass.

3. *Commercial paper.* With an upsurge in commercial paper outstanding, this medium has the dual distinction of being one of the most attractive ways for investing short-term money *and* one of the most *potentially dangerous* hotbeds in a money panic. Among the multibillion-dollar money funds catering to the general public at the beginning of June 1980, the Daily Cash Accumulation Fund had the most, with 86 percent of its assets invested, followed by Paine Webber Cashfund (66 percent) and Rowe Price Prime Reserve (51 percent).

Of course, the portfolio managers of money funds may have the wisdom to shift out of the now-safe-but-dangerous-in-a-money-panic investments at the right time. Then, again, they may not. For this reason, unless you have the time to keep close track of their investment policies and stay ready to move out swiftly when the time comes, you should choose the safest money funds dealing exclusively in Treasury bills.

Rule No. 3. Don't Get Caught In Long Maturities

Although interest rates may drop temporarily between one stage of the panic and the next, the predominant trend will be sharply upward throughout the Great Money Panic. Nevertheless, you will no doubt be continually urged by brokers and bankers to "lock in high yields" for one year or more. Unless you are out to make a capital gain by picking the temporary interest-rate peaks with accuracy, I think you should stay away from all long-term commitments until the panic is over (see end of Book III)—no matter how often people say that "interest rates have peaked."

In order to maximize your yield, I feel you should stay with the shortest possible maturity available. For a saver with ten thousand dollars or more, that would be the three-month Treasury bill, which you can purchase directly at the Treasury's weekly auction or through your broker or bank. For those with more than a hundred thousand dollars even shorter-term Treasury bills and repurchase agreements are readily available.

Money funds, by maintaining an average maturity of as little as two weeks at times, can often help you to maximize your yields. But they can also fall for the lock-in-high-yields psychology, shift their investments out to as much as a full year, suffer minor losses in principal, and, as a result, pass on to you *major* reductions in yield.

It all goes to prove that this is no time to stash your money in what you think is a safe haven and forget about it. Constant vigilance is needed to maximize your safety and income in the tough times ahead.

11

What to Do
with
Your Investments

"THIS BROKERAGE BUSINESS STINKS," shouted George
Bennet one day as he hung onto a strap in the noisy IRT subway
express. "How can anyone ever make a living like this? Volume
dead. Blood all over the floor. Maybe I ought to look for another
job somewhere else. Maybe I ought to join the fifty thousand
brokers who have dropped out of the business. But then again,
damn it, there's gotta be a better way."

That was back in early 1974. By 1980 George Bennet—nick-
named "The Little Big Bear"—was one of the most successful
brokers on Wall Street. How did he do it? Let's listen in on one of
his 1974 phone conversations with a customer and maybe we'll
catch on.

"Bennet here."

"Morning. How did IBM open?"

"Oh, hello, Jack. IBM opened at 240, ran up to 250, and then
crashed to 237. A very big day for IBM."

"How's AT&T?"

"Also weakish. Listen, are you still holding onto that stuff? Why don't you do yourself a favor? Why don't you think seriously about getting rid of your stocks, and getting into Treasury bills. Then you can—"

"Nosiree! Not on your life. You won't get me to sell my IBM or my AT&T for nothing. They've been too good to me over the years. You want me to dump them just like that? Besides, now I've got big paper losses. Why should I make paper losses into *real* losses. Just to pay less taxes? Nosiree! Suppose the market turns around? One of my friends at Merrill just told me yesterday the market's way oversold, said we're due for a big turnaround, a big rally any day now. What do you think?"

"I don't know. Maybe later. Right now it looks pretty bad, but that's just *my* opinion. You're not just going to sit there and watch your stocks sink, are you?"

"No, that's for sure!"

"Well then, here's my suggestion. Say you had a hundred shares of Polaroid when it was going at 130—"

"Yeah? It just so happens I did. So what?"

"OK. Say you sold them and collected the $13,000. And suppose you had second thoughts—that you were going to miss out on a good profit. You could have bought a nine-month 'call'—an option to buy 100 shares any time within nine months at 130. With the call, if the stock went up you would make a profit. If it went down, you would still have your $13,000 minus the $1,500 you paid for the call, minus commission."

"Yeah, great, just great, Monday morning quarterback, twenty-twenty hindsight. What in the world are you telling me this for now? Polaroid's selling at 45. It's all over now."

"OK, but what about IBM—I can sell them for you here or on the next rally, and for $875 I can get you calls that expire in seven months."

"Sorry. It sounds like a gimmick to me. Besides, I just can't sell at these low levels. It would kill me. My wife would kill me."

"All right, then, hold on to your stock. But at least buy some 'puts'—some options to *sell short*. Then you're also covered both ways. You keep the stocks, you still own them, but you're protected just in case the stock goes down, just in case the current trend continues."

The customer, still skeptical, hung up saying he'd talk it over with his wife. Precisely thirty minutes later he called back with an answer.

Selling Short

"Listen, I just had a long talk with my wife. She's against the whole thing. As soon as I mentioned selling short she got all upset. She's against speculation in the stock market in general, but she's even more against selling short. She says that if we sell short we'll be doing a disservice to our country. She says we'll be selling the country short. She says it's wrong, morally wrong. And you know, I think she's got a point there. So we're holding on to what we've got."

"Wait a minute. This isn't speculation—not in your case. You're not doing it for the quick buck. You're just trying to protect yourself against possible losses. You're just buying *a hedge against uncertainty,* one thing we have no shortage of nowadays. Besides, selling short can only help correct imbalances in the marketplace. In the long run it's usually *good* for the country."

"How's that?"

The broker leaned back in his chair and watched the electronic ticker tape flash by. "Selling short is nothing mystical or Machiavellian. It's merely reversing the common order of things. First, you sell something you've borrowed, then later you buy it back. Suppose there is a tremendous oversupply of stock hanging over the market—hoards of potential sellers waiting on the sidelines and only a few individuals in the market buying. Then a lot of short-selling could precipitate a decline in prices—not cause a decline, just precipitate a decline. The people waiting on the sidelines come in and dump their stock once and for all and get it over with, clean out the cobwebs."

"That's good for the marketplace?"

"Wait. Now comes the main benefit. If sellers really panic and stocks go down too far, the short sales outstanding become a cushion, a mechanism that can slow down the decline, spark a rally, and give people a chance to take a breather. The market falls to, say, 550 or 600 on the Dow and the short-sellers say: 'This is it! This is the bottom!' And they take their profits by 'buying in' their short positions, by giving orders to buy the stock. That pushes prices up and gets a temporary rally going, like the battery in the starter motor of an automobile, a reserve of power that can set off a chain reaction of buying."

"So you wait for things to go bad and then you make a profit. That's wrong, I think."

"Bad? Come on. This has nothing to do with good or bad. Take commodities, for instance. If you sell-short wheat futures, you make money when there is *good* news—good weather or good crops. There's an oversupply, and prices go down. It's the selling short now going on *outside* the marketplaces that could be construed as having a negative effect on the economy. More and more people are doing it every day—maybe even your wife."

George asked his customer if he was hoarding anything and discovered that the customer's wife was saving silver quarters and sugar in large quantities.

"What's wrong with that?" the customer added.

"Nothing wrong. In fact, she could make a handsome profit. My point is that she is, in effect, selling *the dollar* short, that's all. On the other hand, even this kind of selling short can have a functional value in the long run. The mass movement toward the accumulation of strategic resources sweeping the Western world has effectively built into the system a high degree of self-sufficiency at the household level. This in turn will provide residual support to the system in the wake of an economic decline. Therefore, selling short the dollar *now* could actually be *good* for the dollar later."

The Little Big Bear went on to explain how "put" options and selling short, if made accessible to the general public, could become "a major evolutionary advance" for the market. The customer said he'd confer with his wife once again and hung up.

Six years went by. Finally, when Bennet thought he'd never hear from the customer again, he showed up one day in person.

Bonds

"I've spent the last six years studying bonds. All that trouble, all that research, and what good did it do me? It got me stuck, that's what. The soaring interest rates killed me. Had I stuck with Treasury bills, as you told me to do, I would be in good shape, but I was sold a bill of goods on tax-exempt revenue bonds, deep-discount corporate bonds, mortgage bonds, you name it. Now that I look back, it's hard for me to believe how ignorant I was. I used to think that Treasury bills and Treasury bonds were the same thing. I didn't realize that the price on the bonds could fall so sharply when interest rates went up."

"The first thing you should do is clean out your portfolio. I wouldn't try to do it on your own, though. Let me handle it for you, and I'll do my best to catch an intermediate rally so that I can get the best prices and help you minimize your losses. It looks to me as if interest rates are going to soar, and all long-term bond prices are going down still further, way down, some tax exempts to forty or fifty; long-term corporate bonds may be cut in half at least."

The customer decided to bring up some of the reasons given him by other brokers why he should *not* sell his bonds. "Suppose I say that I don't care, that I can wait. When the bonds mature I get *all* my money back—no matter what, right? How can I lose? It's guaranteed."

"*Corporate* bonds aren't guaranteed by anyone except the corporation. How do you know which ones are going to survive this crisis? And the chances of default on some revenue bonds are even greater. Besides, after the decline there will be plenty of bargains and opportunities coming up to switch into. You'll want to buy something else and you may end up selling your bonds at a price lower than today. Then again you need the money in your business."

"OK. I'll sell my corporate bonds immediately. But my government-agency bonds—Federal Home Loan, Fannie Mae, Federal Intermediate Credit Bank—are backed by the good faith and credit of the United States Government."

"The faith, maybe; the credit, I'm not so sure. These are relatively independent agencies backed only indirectly by the Government. They're not direct obligations of the U.S. Treasury. Besides, they own mortgages primarily, and these are the first to go sour in the kind of housing-and-construction decline we're having now."

"OK. OK. But my long-term Government bonds. They're good, right?"

"Yes, they're good."

"At least I did *something* right."

"They're good, but not right now. I can see thirty-year Government bond yields hitting 20 percent because of—"

"Hyperinflation?"

"No, because of distress selling by illiquid bond-owners and massive borrowing by the Government. Then, depending on market conditions, you may want to buy them again at highly depressed prices."

"You're driving me up the wall. Stocks are no good! Bonds are no good! How can I make any money?"

Recommended Strategy

"First, I would recommend you sell all assets you do not need to maintain the kind of life you personally want to lead. That may include real estate such as condominiums, a summer house, or even your own home if you and your wife happen to view it as an investment rather than as the place you really want to live."

"What's wrong with real estate?"

"It's a bubble. You should read the 1979 book *The Coming Real-Estate Collapse* by John English and Gray Cardiff. That will tell you why it's a house of cards. The careful sale of your business may also be an excellent way to raise cash, assuming, of course, you'd be equally content in some other activity. This only you can decide."

"Wait—a—minute! My business is depression proof. I'm in the fast-food business. No matter what happens, people still have to eat, don't they?"

"There's no such thing as a depression-proof business. When a panic hits, spending is cut across the board. Everyone gets hurt. However, when it comes to pure investments such as stocks, bonds, or commodities, you should certainly not hesitate to clean out on the first opportunity."

"OK. So let's say I load up with cash. Now what do I do? Let the value of my money sink into oblivion with rampant inflation year after year?"

"We've come to a major crossroads, and you have to make a choice. Either you pay the small price of keeping your money absolutely safe while inflation continues, or you risk huge losses and being wiped out by a deflationary bust. I suggest you do the following: First, keep 85 to 90 percent of your cash in the shortest-term Treasury bills you can buy."

The customer was a bit frustrated. "Treasury bills! I want something I can sink my teeth into. I want something solid. When I buy Treasury bills, all I get is a receipt. Besides, if things are going to get so bad as you say, what makes you so sure the Treasury bills won't go bad too?"

The Little Big Bear had spent the better part of his adult life considering this kind of question. "If one believes that the United States will continue to exist as a sovereign nation, you should have no doubt that Treasury bills—the prime obligation of the U.S. Government and backed by the sweat and blood of 220 million Americans—will remain intact regardless of any economic or political crisis. If, on the other hand, you come out and say that a default on three-month Treasury securities is a real possibility, you also have to stand by the relatively absurd statement that your country is coming to an end within the next ninety days. Let's get back to the real world. I suggest you stick with the shortest possible T-bills, shifting into the six-month bills whenever interest rates reach a temporary peak."

"How will I know?"

"I'll give you the signal whenever possible. So far I've caught every major turn."

"Oh, good!"

"Second, keep the remaining 10 or 15 percent of your cash in our money fund for moving in and out of interest-rate futures. They are the ideal medium for profiting from the coming crisis."

"Interest-rate futures?"

"Right. They're U.S. Treasury securities or U.S. agency bonds traded in pools of $100,000 on the Chicago Board of Trade (CBT) and in $1 million units for T-bills on the International Monetary Market of the Chicago Mercantile Exchange, known as the IMM. They're listed every day in your *Wall Street Journal* under the heading 'Futures Prices,' and you can buy them—or sell them short—like any commodity."

"Where?"

"Right here. I can handle them for you. Or you can go to any broker who handles commodities. It has become one of the most active markets we've got."

"What do I do?"

"I think you should sell them short, especially the Ginnie Maes, bonds of the General National Mortgage Association (GNMA). I think they will fall the most sharply in price because of fundamental weaknesses in the mortgages that back them."

"What's the profit potential?"

"Let's say you put up $3,000 for a short sale of the Ginnie Maes of March 1981, and you get in at the current price of 76. And let's say interest rates in general go back to their old peaks reached in March 1980. That would indicate a price of about 67. Personally I think this Ginnie Mae is headed for 50 or lower. But let's say you decide to take profits at 67. You'd make nine points, or $9,000 per contract—a gain of 300 percent on the money you put up.

"I hasten to add that, if interest rates suddenly go down sharply and you're not on the ball, the risk of loss is also great. But let me also say this: My customers have made substantial profits with this strategy *despite* the continued danger that the Federal Reserve might all of a sudden push interest rates down and bond prices up.

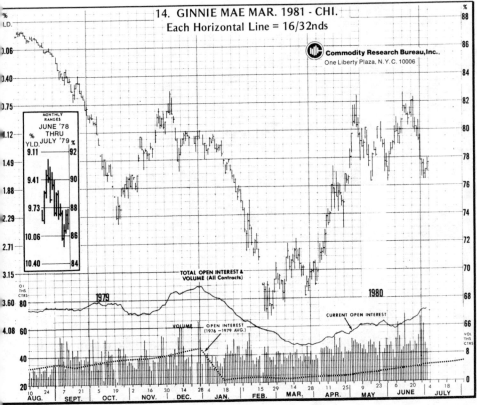

14. GINNIE MAE MAR. 1981 - CHI.
Each Horizontal Line = 16/32nds

Commodity Research Bureau, Inc.,
One Liberty Plaza, N.Y.C. 10006

source: Commodity Research Bureau, New York

Today, even that danger appears to have diminished; the Fed has little elbow room, giving us much more confidence in our analysis of real market forces, and also reducing the risk of unexpected losses."

12

What to Do in Your Business

A FEW WEEKS AFTER the recession began, the chairman of the board of a manufacturing conglomerate by the name of GBO Industries hired a rare bird called "the deflation expert"—a retired executive with a complete repertoire of innovative methods for selling off assets, moving inventories, and mobilizing cash. The chairman, the deflation expert, and a senior economist from the corporate planning department met in the plush sitting room adjoining the chairman's office.

"What have you done so far?" was the expert's first question.

"We have cut production 10 percent, and we're trying as hard as possible to float a new bond issue. But it doesn't look too good at present, because Uncle Sam is crowding us out. We're something like twentieth on line, and the traffic is almost at a standstill."

"How much did you say you're cutting production? Only 10 percent? Get me all the latest facts and figures on your operation schedule—sales, costs, the works—also all up-to-the-minute financial data. We had better get this thing moving, and fast."

The chairman nodded deliberately.

"What's your liquidity ratio?" asked the deflation expert.

"Liquidity? Oh! You mean the—"

"Yes, cash. I want to know how much cash you have on hand to pay up current debts."

"Oh, mayber 15 percent, maybe less now, because we had a decline in sales last week."

"Good, very good. Your liquidity is low, but it could be much worse. You still have a chance."

"A chance to what?"

"A chance to avoid the bankruptcy courts, of course."

The two men were silent as they glanced at each other.

"What do you suggest?"

"First, raise more cash—mobilize it from overseas, get it from customers, sell off some of that inventory, rip out phones from the walls if you think it will help, but let's *move!* First stage, 25 percent; second stage, 50 percent; third stage, 75 percent."

"Seventy-five percent of what?" asked the chairman, still bewildered.

"We'll take the first stage right now, the second within thirty to forty-five days, and the third within, say, sixty to ninety days, depending on circumstances. We'll be flexible. Watch the conditions in the marketplace, but take action without hesitation."

"What action? What specifically are we going to do? Seventy-five percent of *what?*" the chairman repeated, more perplexed than ever.

"Cut, sir, cut. Cut everything down to the bone if necessary. Production. Expenses. Personnel. Space. Facilities."

The company economist, who until now had kept his peace, finally interjected. "You're nuts! You can't just cut indiscriminately across the board. You'll ruin us! We'll lose our market share for good, create an uproar with the unions, destroy company morale. Sure, we've had a big bust in consumer spending. But that was just because of artificially high interest rates. Now that interest rates are down, lo and behold, the consumer is spending again."

"Exactly, and now I think interest rates are heading back for their old peaks. Last time the Government punctured the boom. This time they're going to have to *sabotage the incipient recovery.*

Anyhow, who said we'd cut indiscriminately? We'll begin with the excess fat."

The Contraction Plan

"So what's your plan?" asked the economist, with a heavy overtone of skepticism.

"In the first phase you concentrate on current assets. Sell all stocks and bonds in the investment portfolio. Call an emergency meeting with the union to warn them of the coming crisis. Let them know that we're sending word to the bank to liquidate all securities in the pension fund in order to protect employees from stock and bond market losses. We want cash."

"What about receivables?" asked the company economist.

"Contact all your big customers. Give them a special bonus anywhere up to 15 percent for any and all payments made within the next fortnight. Give them 20 percent if necessary. Get that cash in now! Next on my list is inventory. What's your inventory situation?"

"We have one month of semifinished and finished goods, and forty-five days of raw materials and commodities, but, as you said, I've seen it build up without warning before, and it's beginning to do it again now. We see it in our durable goods."

"Sell the excesses! It doesn't matter how you sell them, just sell. There are still quite a few buyers around, but we must slash prices, and I don't mean the rebate gimmick. When you slash prices, make up your mind to keep prices down, eliminating from your product line any low-profit items that can't stand the pressure. You must act before it's too late."

"Before it's too late?"

"Before your competitors start dumping *their* inventories, and you can't sell yours no matter how much you cut prices. It's the same logic you used during the boom when you were trying to expand faster than the other guy. Except this time it's contraction, not expansion."

For five minutes the economist had been silent, making calculations on his yellow pad. Suddenly his eyes lit up, and he began talking about items like bankers' acceptances, commercial paper, certificates of deposit, high-yielding corporate bonds. He had discovered that the average yield on these investment mediums was greater than GBO's average return on plant and equipment; that they could make more money simply by raising cash and putting it to work somewhere else.

"Not on your life," responded the deflation expert. "Don't you see? Those bankers' acceptances, commercial paper, and what have you are backed up by the very same goods we are trying to get rid of ourselves—the inventory stashed away in the warehouses, the receivables, the obsolete production facilities. There's only one place this cash is going—good old short-term Treasury bills."

"You mean those ninety-day Treasury bills that have fluctuated so wildly in rate recently?"

"No, I do not. Ninety-day bills are all right for individuals, but we're talking now about $200 million. You can afford to keep two full-time money experts on this and buy the Treasury bills in the secondary market. Get thirty-, ten- or even five-day maturities, depending on the interest-rate outlook."

"We already *have* a cash-management person!"

"Yes. But now what you need is a Treasury-bill management person—a real specialist in government markets, and a crackerjack interest-rate forecaster."

"All Treasury bills are safe. So what's the difference?"

"They are all safe. But with interest rates in a fast, upward swing, we stick to the shortest-term—one-week or even one-day— paper to take advantage of the higher rates immediately as they show up. Then, if we think rates will be coming down for a short time, we move into the ninety-day bills. Finally, when we think it's all over, we start looking at the longer-term stuff. Six-month bills. Treasury notes. Bonds."

"Aren't you jumping ahead a bit? What about the second phase?"

Phase two involved some real cutting and called for longer-range planning. The expert took the stand that the superboom of the seventies was no more a representative of "normal times" than the depression years. First he requested a GBO sales graph that ran from the founding of the corporation to the present. With a red pen he crossed off everything after 1969 and drew a trend line under the sales curve from 1946. Finally, he drew a circle around the point where the trend line intercepted with the present. It was about the level reached in 1973.

"Of course this is merely a rough 'guesstimate,' but it will give you some idea of the average market for your products that you can expect over the coming years. You say, 'This is the level we can expect to rally back to as soon as the panic is over. This is our nucleus.' Then be prepared to see everything else cut away, at least temporarily."

The deflation expert flipped through the corporate records he had been studying carefully for the past two weeks. He picked out a factory in Dayton, Ohio, with extremely high overhead expenses, which concentrated on products well outside GBO's area of specialization and had a long history of poor quality control.

"Here's a good example," he said. "It's been sitting around bringing you nothing but headaches for the past ten years and very little revenue for two years, right? Well, unless you can turn it into a money-maker right now, I say get rid of it. Bring in some cash and transfer some of its operations to other plants you have in Cleveland."

"OK. That makes sense."

"Then there's this other one in New Jersey."

"Hey, wait a minute! That's good stuff. That plant was our prize, our brainchild," protested the economist.

"Sure, sure, maybe in the past, but it's a burden now. No revenues. It's gotta go! Sell it!"

"All right," said the chairman. "I see your point. I wouldn't have hired you if I didn't see big trouble ahead."

"But labor won't stand for it," cried the economist. "They'll murder us with strikes."

"That's something you've got to cope with. You have to make every possible effort to soften the blow to the employees, look out for their welfare, even if it does cost you something. You tell labor this: 'If we do this now, we have a chance of surviving and of hiring you back as soon as we're over the hump. But if we wait, there's a chance we're going under. Then you'd *really* be unemployed.'"

"You mean we scare them—like you're scaring me now," said the chairman.

"It's either now or never. If you give them plenty of advance warning, you'll be able to use the interim period for planning ways to provide for their emergency needs. When they see others in your industry laying off workers without any compassion whatsoever, then they'll understand."

"When in the world is this nightmare going to end?" asked the chairman, throwing up his arms in exasperation.

"You haven't heard about phase three yet."

"What's that? Set a fire and collect the insurance?" the chairman said with a nervous laugh.

"No," replied the expert, still quite serious. "Many insurance companies would probably be broke by then too. Phase three is the 75 percent phase. You close down most of the plants, keeping on a skeleton crew, just enough to keep your pulse going. Like hibernation."

The chairman had been with the GBO for decades, was one of the largest stockholders and identified closely with the company. To slash that deep was like amputating his own legs.

"Now you're really talking suicide. So far I've gone along with this. But to close down? That's just more than we can tolerate."

"Here are your alternatives: either to close down most of your plants ahead of time or close down *all* of your plants later on. If you do the former, you stay alive and can start opening up ahead of everyone else, even make big inroads into the market. If you take the second alternative and you're forced to close down when you're not ready for it, you may never open up again."

The chairman and the company economist could take no more and without further ado closed the meeting by asking the deflation expert to leave. Once he was gone, the two men let out sighs of relief.

"What an idiot! But I think we should follow his advice on one economy measure at least," commented the economist.

"What's that?"

"Don't send the bastard his check if he bills us for all this nonsense."

The two men returned to the "real world of corporate expansion, profits, and stock dividends." For one week nothing happened, and the deflation expert was forgotten completely. Two weeks later sales fell 30 percent and earnings 98 percent—the sharpest month-to-month drop ever recorded in the firm's history. There appeared in GBO—and in many companies like it—a *cash hole*, a great pit into which cash disappeared and never reappeared again. Inventories, which they thought were under control, suddenly ballooned from one month's supply to three months'.

"What's happened?" cried the chairman in utter frenzy.

"We *expected* a drop. I'm telling you. But we didn't expect it to happen so fast. Our timing was off, that's all."

"*That's all?* Well the timing of our *creditors* isn't off. They want us to pay our debts. On time."

Late that evening the economist found himself canceling a date with his girlfriend and instead dictating a letter to the deflation expert. He pressed down the record/play button on his minicassette machine and spoke: "Dear Mr. Hack: Please allow me to express my sincere regrets for our initial skepticism regarding your contraction plan; it was a lot of tough medicine to swallow in one gulp. In the past couple of weeks, however, we have had a better opportunity to think it over more carefully and have come to the conclusion that we would like to develop it further and put it into practice as soon as possible. We look forward to meeting with you at your earliest convenience. Sincerely."

13

The Debate Between
Mr. Bald
and Mr. Beard

EXCEPT PERHAPS FOR the festivities between sessions, banking conventions were dull affairs. But this one, held in St. Louis during the initial stages of the money panic, was no ordinary convention. Most bankers greeted old friends with a solemnity appropriate for funerals, as bond markets collapsed and last year's promises by money experts that "interest rates had peaked out" began to sound like a practical joke clipped out of last Sunday's "Peanuts" comic strip.

First, Pennsylvania had lost billions speculating in U.S. Government securities and was rumored to be in bad shape. Who would have thought, only several months ago, that the prime obligation of the *United States Treasury* would one day be associated with *speculation?* At the same time, some savings and loans were refusing delivery on Ginnie Mae futures they had bought, because, unless they did renege on the deal, it would wipe out their capital. Who would ever have imagined years ago that established financial institutions would renege on a solid market agreement?

In the large convention hall one speaker after another came up to the podium, talked about the need to fight inflation, made a few noncommittal comments on the possible squeeze on bank earnings, and finally wound up with an optimistic note calling for cooperation. The audience began to fidget and cough, and a fat man in the front row had obviously fallen asleep. No one wanted to set off any sparks. Everyone wanted to get it over with and go home. But the program wasn't finished.

It was Mr. Bald's turn to speak. A short, fragile-looking man over seventy years of age, weighing less than 125 pounds, he was one of the few remaining old-style conservative bankers. Some bankers thought Mr. Bald was too old to run a bank. Others were convinced he had simply lost his marbles. But on this day of reckoning everyone was extremely anxious to hear what he had to say. As he began to speak, he put up a chart with a title in bold red lettering: THE STRUCTURE OF DISINTERMEDIATION.

In past conventions he usually did a little jig on the podium and gave a gloom-and-doom sermon on the coming bank collapse. But now that some of his predictions about disintermediation—a shift of savings from banks to Treasury bills and money funds—had actually begun to take place, his statement was brief and his tone matter of fact.

"The chart behind me shows changes in our Savings Forecaster Index. It is derived from a survey conducted by our bank once a week to (a) evaluate saver opinion and savings plans, (b) project savings flow, and (c) attempt to determine what kind of savers are making withdrawals. As you can see, this barometer has anticipated fluctuations in savings flows faithfully. Last month it fell through the floor. Conclusion: The disintermediation crisis will soon spread from the thrifts to the commercial banks. In view of the refusal on the part of most city banks to take protective action, our bank has taken the following steps: (1) early recall of cash reserves from the federal funds market; (2) early disposal of participation loans from large city banks; and (3) all other actions deemed necessary in order to cut the umbilical cord to the city banks and achieve a high level of real self-reliance for the immediate future."

For a moment the bankers froze on the edge of their seats, but a few seconds later, they burst into a prolonged wave of whispering and murmuring. Finally, one of the most influential city bankers present, a Mr. Beard from Chicago, rose to his feet and raised his hand in protest. The man's outward calm masked his anger and frustration.

"Mr. Bald, how can you get up there on that platform in this atmosphere charged with apprehension, in this convention that is supposed to strengthen interbank ties, and tell us coldly that you want to 'sever the umbilical cord'? You're saying in effect you want to ditch us, abandon your correspondent bank in the city. Precisely when we need each other the most, precisely when *you* need *us* the most, you're saying you're going to crawl into a shell?"

Mr. Bald refused to be intimidated. "We're just cleaning our own house, protecting our own assets. Tell me, Mr. Beard, why should we get enmeshed in your problems? Give me one good reason why we should suffer for your mistakes."

"Mistakes? What mistakes?" answered the city banker with growing impatience.

"Franklin National-type mistakes. U.S. National of San Diego-type mistakes. First Pennsylvania-type errors. Demonstrate to us that these banks were indeed the exception and not the rule and I will retract everything I have said so far."

"You're missing the whole point, Mr. Bald. Those are the exceptions that prove the rule. Even though some banks *have* gone under, the system survived *and thrived*. Granted we will see a lot of changes coming to the banking system in the 1980s, some of them perhaps rather drastic changes. I can see big competition for new consumer banking services. I can see big problems for banks who can't afford the cost of the new interest-bearing checking accounts. I can see minibanks digging out little niches in specialized electronic bill-paying services. And I can see superbanks gobbling up many of the minibankers. But most important, woe on those who are caught up in old-style banking—like you, Mr. Bald."

"*You're* missing the point, Mr. Beard. *First,* we clean out all the mess, shave away all the bad loans from the good loans. *Then* we bring in the new services groomed to the *real* need of the saver—safety."

"Who are you to sit there in judgment on what is good and what is bad?"

"That's not my decision. Bad are all those paraphernalia we have accumulated which are today maladapted to the realities of our environment. My question is this: How many more Franklin Nationals are there around? What assurance do we have from your bank or any other big city bank that it can't happen to you?" The old man paused for a moment to let the words sink in, and then continued. "Look at all those real estate investment trusts you talked us into buying in the early 1970s! Many of them went broke, and you asked us not to rock the boat. All I can tell you is that you fellows were lucky. Real estate recovered and bailed you out. *But did you learn from your mistakes?* No! Let me ask you this, Mr. Beard. How many more rotten apples are there in your barrel of loans and investments? In state loans? In loans to the big cities? In loans to the less developed countries? To Chryslers? How many dinosaurs are *you* feeding, Mr. Beard?"

By this time the city banker was red in the face, and the others in the audience were in an uproar. No one had ever heard that kind of language at a banking convention. Cuss words, yes, but long tirades against an influential colleague were taboo. Nevertheless, the debate between Mr. Beard and Mr. Bald continued.

Mr. Beard once again raised his voice. "Have the city banks ever conked out on any loans with your bank? Have we ever reneged on any federal funds? Haven't you always received your interest every single month? Haven't you gotten the fees that were due you?"

The city banker turned to the audience. "I want it to be clear for the record that our bank has never taken any action that would warrant this panic policy Mr. Bald is advocating today. This man is trying to push the panic button. Luckily for us, he's the only one, because, if there were a few more bankers like him, they could bring down the whole system." Then again, turning to Mr. Bald: "Your name is Mr. *Bald,* not Mr. Judas. Remember that!"

Mr. Bald responded with a calm tone but harsh words as he shook his finger at the younger Mr. Beard. "Don't tell me how to run my bank, and I won't tell you how to run yours. All we want is to have the money ready to meet the big withdrawals we see coming. We need that money *before* it happens, not *after* it happens. That's all."

Mr. Beard, the city banker, could take no more. He muttered a few last comments under his breath and stormed out of the room. With his departure most of the sting of the protest against Mr. Bald was gone, and the meeting settled down to a more orderly question-and-answer period. The first question came from a Mr. Mascot, a small-town banker from the heart of the wheat-growing region of his state.

"Our bank has substantial losses in tax-exempt municipal bonds, as I think all banks have. What have you done about *your* tax exempts?"

The old man smiled. For the first time in many years someone was asking him his opinion without any sign of sarcasm.

"We sold the municipal bonds. We bit the bullet and took the losses. We sold off 40 percent in the fall of 1974 rally, and we sold most of the rest before the October 1979 'Volcker Massacre.' We're trying to get rid of the tail end of them now. First, we shifted from long-term tax exempts to short-term tax-exempts. Then we shifted from short-term tax exempts to Treasury bills. Now we realize that once we started on the liquidity path, we should have gone all the way through without hesitation. Fast. We also got out of our mortgages early in the game. We were one of the first to offer homeowners big discounts on their mortgages if they paid up ahead of time—until, of course, they figured out the arithmetic of it and realized it wasn't such a bargain after all."

The man who asked the question was still puzzled. "How did you juggle the losses on the books? God only knows how many times we talked about selling those bad municipals. But there was always that one big obstacle in the way—the stockholders. The stockholders would be up in arms if we sold the municipals, if we showed losses on our books. They'd be on our necks day and night, screaming, 'What happened to your earnings?' Then an even bigger obstacle reared its ugly head—low capital position. If we cleaned out all our municipals tomorrow, we'd be finished. Down the drain. How did you handle *your* stockholders?"

"You've got to level with them. If you don't tell them the truth, you're just postponing the inevitable. They're going to find out about the losses sooner or later, anyhow, so what's the difference? Also, look what happened to the stock prices of Morgan, Citicorp, Chase. Did it do any good to show big earnings? No, the stocks fell apart anyway. Why? Because many stockholders are knowledge-able, sophisticated investors and know more about the hidden problems in the banks than you think they do. If we give them the bad news ahead of the bad events, at least they'll know the score, and perhaps there will be less panic selling when our earnings do go down. Listen to this. In our bank, some of them came to our support. After we told them the whole story, some of them even called in the next day, said they understood what we were doing, and that they'd hold onto their stock come hell or high water. They said they have confidence in us."

As soon as he finished, half a dozen hands popped up around the room. It was beginning to look like a Presidential news conference. Mr. Bald called on a woman banker at the far end of the room.

"You're a very lucky man," she said. "You stayed away from those participation loans right from the beginning. You made only 'depression-proof' loans. But we weren't so smart. Our bank has five million of a four-year loan to International Harvester that First of Detroit got us into. We think it could go sour. We want to sell the loan, but even if we could get a buyer for it, Detroit has strongly implied to us—or, rather, gently threatened us—that if we try to sell out, we'll stir up a storm. They said that they would take retaliatory action against us, that our bank would be black-balled. So what do we do?"

"You want an honest answer? The way I see it, Harvester could go under. So you really have only two choices. Kiss the five million loan good-bye and get one swollen black eye or stick up for your rights and get blackballed. That's your choice. A black eye or a blackball. If it were my choice, I'd sell off the loan at a small loss and forget all the niceties. This is no longer just a matter of getting a black eye. I think those banks could wind up dragging you down into a black hole."

The next question came from a tall man with horn-rimmed glasses sitting up front.

"You're selling loans, right? You're selling off investments, right? You're getting people to close out mortgages, right? So what you're actually doing is contracting your business, cutting down. My question is, after you've done all that, what do you have left? How can you pay interest on deposits when you're cutting off all that income? If we did that in our bank, we would have nothing left for paying the highly inflated operating costs. We'd be deep in the red. Isn't your bank in the red too, Mr. Bald?"

Mr. Bald beamed with pride. "We—are—making—a—profit," he said, punctuating each word with the tap of his forefinger on the podium. "We took the extra cash from mortgages plus the proceeds from the sales of loans and investments, and now we're riding the boom in—"

"Boom? What boom? There's no more boom," interrupted a short man jumping to his feet. "You're all wet if you think there's a boom."

"We're riding the boom in *interest rates*," Mr. Bald said, raising his voice. "We're in Treasury bills, remember? While everyone else is terrified of tight money, scared silly of the liquidity crisis, we welcome it. *Every time short-term rates go up, we get more income.* Besides, we never went overboard in our costs. Computers, yes. But fancy executive office buildings? Penthouse restaurants? Big colorful fountains? That's for the birds, the supermen and the superstars. We're just ordinary bankers. Business volume is off now, but we *expected* business volume to be off. We planned for it, and we cut costs accordingly."

There was time for one last question before the next speaker came on. It was Mr. Mascot again.

"It seems to me that you are leading your bank down the road of stagnation—and perhaps extinction; that your bank will just dwindle over the years and peter out. But even if it doesn't, how will you ever grow?"

"What are our plans for the future? We're preparing for the future by holding onto our depositors."

"Are you stating that you have finally found a gimmick to stop withdrawals? That's hard to believe, because we have tried everything. We've used the six-month money market certificates. We tried intercepting withdrawals with a friendly chat. We tried implied threats of invoking our delaying right. We even used the fine print on CDs to make outright refusals! Now that we look back, though, it's becoming more and more obvious that we would have been much better off if we had just kept our mouths shut. As soon as we tried to attach strings, as soon as we put up even the smallest obstacle against withdrawals, the word spread through the town like wildfire, and we wound up getting still more people asking for their money. How come *your* gimmick worked and ours didn't?"

"I think you misunderstood me. We made absolutely no effort to hold onto the money itself in passbook or checking accounts. Anyone who made a sizable withdrawal received a call from our staff within twenty-four hours. We made no mention of the withdrawal. We informed each depositor that the bank was willing to provide a special personalized service through which he could purchase high-yielding Treasury bills. We told him that these Treasury bills would be segregated from all the other bank assets and that the Federal Reserve receipts would be kept safe for him in a special Treasury-bill vault. This plan has been very successful. Almost 80 percent of the money withdrawn from our regular accounts is now in our vaults. In addition, since we were the only ones providing this service in the entire county, we attracted new customers. More important, we're in touch with our old customers, and there's a good chance we'll get them back into our regular accounts when our own bank's interest rates become competitive again. To make a long story short, we're going to survive, that's for certain. We're going to survive this crisis."

14

Gold
and Silver

"I HAVE MADE a fortune in inflation hedges," said a close friend as he sat down in an armchair. "In 1970 I bought gold at $36.41, sold out at $680, and am back in again with an average of about $550. I bought ASA for $2½ and took some profits yesterday at 80. I'm holding several sets of three of the Graf Zeppelin stamps, which sold for about $400 to $500 in 1970 and have recently reached a peak of about $10,000—not to mention my 1913 Indian gold pieces, which have gone up *one hundred times* from $135 to $13,500! What do you think?"

"Most inflation hedges," I explained, "will be hurt by deflation. But there's more to this than inflation or deflation, especially when it comes to the free market price of gold. The OPEC nations alone have accumulated a surplus of $115 billion, a small portion of which can easily bid up the price of gold bullion in the event of a geopolitical crisis—I have in mind particularly the Mideast and West Asia. In that event, silver will tend to follow suit. But if I were you, I wouldn't bet on it. The economic fundamentals point to a substantial decline in the price of all precious metals."

"What are you talking about?" he queried, raising his voice to a higher octave. "A politician is a politician is a politician. When backed up against the wall, he will flood the world with fiat money, create hyperinflation, and eventually destroy all the normal trappings of civilization as we know it."

"The inflation game is nearly up," I countered.

"Why? Give me one good reason!"

Like many laymen and experts, my friend failed to grasp the real meaning of the bond-market collapse. I told him how, at one point in February 1980, *it became next to impossible for the Government to borrow and how any efforts by the Federal Reserve to provide the funds merely made the collapse that much worse.* "The bond-market collapse is the missing link between inflation and deflation."

"The missing link?"

"Exactly. In the great inflation-deflation debate it was always agreed that the inflationary boom would at some time or another trigger a deflationary bust. The big argument, however, was always *when.* The answer is now clear: It's when bond-owners and other creditors become so sensitive to inflationary signals that they dump their holdings and cause sharp price declines—first in bonds, and then in stocks or commodities." To make sure my point was absolutely clear, I drew it out for him on a napkin:

Inflation ——→ Bond-market Collapse ——→ Deflation

"For years," I continued, "politicians have pump-primed the economy with big budget deficits, borrowed the money from the public, stimulated more inflation, and then paid back with cheaper currency; and for years the public fell for it. But no more. Early this year, when the Government couldn't borrow in the marketplace, the politicians were faced with two and only two choices: default or *deflate.* Deflation might mean defeat in the next election; but default would imply an immediate end to their political careers, the end of the Administration, and ultimately the end of the Government itself. Even the most political of politicians chose—and will continue to choose—deflation as the lesser of the evils."

My friend was still not convinced. "But what about the wheel-barrow inflation of Weimar Germany in the 1920s? What about the triple-digit inflation of Brazil or Argentina?"

"Germany had no bond markets to speak of in those days. Nor do any of the developing countries today. The only nations with fully developed bond markets are the U.S., West Germany, Britain, and Japan—perhaps France. *All,* without exception, have been repeatedly forced to take relatively strong anti-inflation measures whenever wholesale or consumer prices rose sharply.

"Moreover, the primary cause of the German hyperinflation was the physical destruction of productive capacity, the paralyzation of the rolling stock, and the removal of a large percentage of the workers from the labor force. The primary cause of inflation in third world countries is rooted in the imbalances and distortions of 'underdevelopment'—an excessive dependence upon capital imports from the industrial nations and a premature stimulation of urban, industrial growth.

"Unlike the German economy of the twenties, the productive capacity of the industrialized world is at an all-time high, churning out in the year 1979 an estimated $7¼ trillion in goods and services per year, slightly under $20 billion per day, $830 million per hour! And unlike Brazil's finance minister Delfim Netto, the U.S. Secretary of the Treasury can't run off to foreign banks to meet most of his borrowing needs."

"OK," he said, "so we have deflation. So what? Granted, silver and some other inflation hedges might suffer, but gold will naturally benefit from any uncertainty, whether deflation or inflation. The proof is what happened in 1934. The U.S. Government raised its gold price by 75 percent to $35 an ounce. This time it appears they'll raise the price of gold to $2,000 an ounce or more. How else are they going to solve the international liquidity crisis?"

"That's the same argument Jacques Rueff offered several years ago. Subsequently, he changed his mind; he came to the realization that raising the price of gold would only reduce certain *international* debts. It would have little or no effect upon the real problem—domestic debts. Double the price of gold, triple it. Add three zeros. General Motors will still owe the banks a billion dollars; and that billion dollars won't be any easier to refinance than before."

We spent the rest of the evening going over the reasons why I think rapid deflation and soaring interest rates are imminent.

Reason #1. Hidden Market Forces

Which market force is more powerful: the demand for *"goods"* or the demand for *"money,"* the need for more material things or the need for cash and credit? Normally, economists answer this question in terms of the "flows," the new supplies and demands coming into the market at any given moment in time, the current availability and needs for cash or commodities coming into the field of vision. But these were no longer normal times. Hidden supplies of goods and hidden demands for money *accumulated over the years* may suddenly appear on the market.

Because of the universal fear of rising prices there was an equally universal hoarding of material goods by families and businesses—freezers full of meat, shrimp, and vegetables; sacks of gold coins, silver quarters, and antiques; inventories of cars, appliances, toys, and photographic equipment; stockpiles of lumber, cotton, copper, steel, petrochemicals, and petroleum—all considered a hedge against inflation. On the other hand, as we have seen repeatedly, a potentially overwhelming demand for money existed, stemming from the cash shortages of major corporations, banks, and governments. There is no direct way of measuring these hidden supplies and demands, but the accompanying table contains rough estimates based primarily upon available inventory and liquidity statistics.

The left side of this "balance sheet" (the supply of goods) shows that, as of mid-1980 corporations had $734 billion in inventories plus $285 billion in future commitments to suppliers. (Sears alone had some $2½ billion in inventories and over $4 billion in future commitments.) Consumers owned an estimated $700 billion in automobiles and appliances alone, 25 percent of which were excess

TABLE 8
The Hidden Forces Behind the Money Panic

	Billions of dollars	
Sector	Hidden supply of goods	Hidden demand for money
Corporations	734	670
Consumers	2,395	—
Banks	—	62
TOTAL	3,129	732

excess or out of tune with real, environmentally determined needs.

The right column (demand for money) shows that nonfinancial corporations had a deficit or hidden demand of $670 billion ($134 billion in cash and equivalent minus $804 billion in short-term liabilities). Banks and thrift institutions had $310 billion in cash and equivalent, but $372 billion in short-term liabilities, leaving a "deficit" of $62 billion.

In all, there was a residual supply of an estimated $3,129 billion in goods and residual demand of $732 billion for money overhanging the marketplace. As a result, during the Great Money Panic the prices of most goods were unstable and ready to fall, while the price of money was highly volatile and ready to skyrocket.

Reason #2. The Credit Printing Presses Are Slowing Down

Much has been said about the money printing presses in Washington. But they were small in comparison with the giant network of printing presses located in every bank, in every large corporation, and in every seat of government. The banks printed credit money in the form of mortgages and all kinds of loans. The corporations printed commercial paper, bonds, and notes. Everyone was in the credit-printing business. Graph 15, based on the Flow of Funds statistics provided by the Federal Reserve, represents the grand total of all net new credit—or debts—created in the U.S. This should not be confused with the *accumulation* of debts outstanding. It is, rather, the amount *added* every year onto the debt pyramid.

In Nixon's days, in 1970, new credit was running at an average rate of $106 billion a year; by the third quarter of 1979 it had reached an annual rate of $538 billion, a jump of over five times in less than ten years. It is this great boom in credit that has brought us price inflation, the near collapse of the dollar, and the rise of gold and silver. It is the great credit machine you see in this graph that was the real source of most of your profits in inflation hedges, single-family homes, and—to a greater degree than you might suspect—in your business as well. In order to maintain the momentum of the inflationary boom, it would have been necessary to

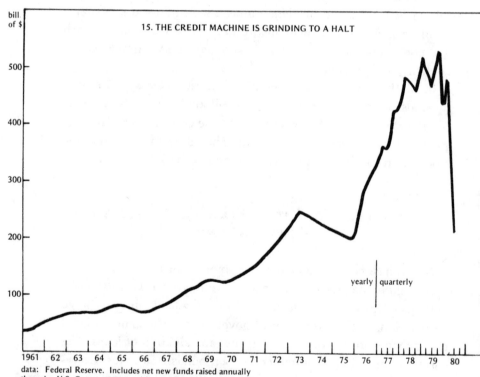

15. THE CREDIT MACHINE IS GRINDING TO A HALT

data: Federal Reserve. Includes net new funds raised annually
through: U.S. Government securities, state and local bonds, corporate
and foreign bonds, mortgages, consumer credit, bank loans,
open-market paper, and other debt instruments.

continue this rate of increase, creating an additional $600 to $650 billion in new credit every year.

But now look! Credit creation plunged to $217 billion in the second quarter of 1980, an unprecedented 60 percent drop from the peak reached only nine months earlier. The printing presses are grinding to a halt. What does this mean? It means that a deflationary panic is imminent, and that even with the relaxing of credit controls and even assuming a temporary resurgence of new credit, there is little hope of recovering to previous peak levels.

How will events unfold? No one can say for certain. In the fictional sections to follow I shall outline what I believe to be the most likely scenario. As you read these chapters, you may occasionally find yourself wondering what is fact and what is fiction. I have made the distinction as follows:

Fact: Statistics or events, accompanied by specific dates such as "as of March 31, 1980," "by year-end 1979," "in 1929," etc., or by such words as "before the panic" and "during the boom."

Fiction: All materials with no specific time reference.

We now skip forward in time to the days when the bulk of the crisis is over in order to look back on the Great Money Panic from the perspective of a future historian. Please bear in mind that, although we are at times powerless to control *some* events, nothing is entirely inevitable. With advance warning we often retain the ability to mold, to avoid, and, in some cases, prevent the dire events that lie ahead.

BOOK
III

The
Panic

THE CITY BANKS WERE HIT FROM TWO SIDES

15

The Ghosts of the Past

THE GREAT MONEY PANIC was like no other panic or crash in American history.

The panics and slumps of 1833, 1837, and 1857 came on the heels of speculative land booms, stimulated by the advancing railroads and financed by locally printed dollars. The panic of 1901 centered in an attempt to take over the Northern Pacific Railroad, and culminated in a battle between the Morgan-Hill and Harriman-Kuhn-Loeb groups to corner the market and gain control over the railroad. The 1907 collapse, which later became known as the "rich man's panic," followed a speculative spurt in copper stocks and a boom in corporate mergers. The crash of 1920-21 resulted primarily from the postwar accumulation of inventories by large manufacturers, farmers, and speculators. The great crash of 1929 involved a huge stock pyramid built by brokers, banks, utility tycoons, and individuals.

On the surface the Great Money Panic was all of these wrapped up in one; in reality it was none of these.

Like the panics of the 1800s, the Great Money Panic included a major bust in land and real estate. Then thousands of local banks financed the real-estate bubble through the unregulated printing of paper called "money" or "dollars." This time local banks financed the real-estate bubble through the unrestrained printing of paper called "mortgages" and "home improvement loans."

Like 1901, the Great Money Panic was preceded by attempts from powerful corporate groups to gain control over the stocks of major corporations through mergers, raids, and tenders.

As in 1907, the Great Money Panic included speculative booms in metals and commodities. That time it was primarily copper and coffee. This time the boom included gold, silver, sugar, soybeans, and petroleum.

As in 1921, the Great Money Panic caught business by surprise, loaded with inventories and productive capacity. That time it was mostly American auto and tire-makers, sugar producers, and cotton farmers. This time it surprised virtually every manufacturer and distributor in the industrialized world, plus farmers and cattle ranchers.

As in 1929, the Great Money Panic pulled the rug out from under the speculative pyramids in the banking and brokerage industries. That time the debt pyramid centered primarily in brokerage loans, with some as low as 10 percent margin on stocks. This time the debt pyramid had spread into every sector of the economy, *leaving the entire nation on average margins of often less than 10 percent.* Prior to the 1920 and 1929 crises the U.S. had close to $1.50 in gold and foreign-exchange reserves to cover every dollar of liabilities to foreigners; in 1980 it was down to about 10 cents. In 1920 and 1929 the consumer used less than 10 percent of his disposable income for debt repayments, leaving a "net disposable income" of 90 percent or more; in 1975 this measure was down to 82 percent and in 1980 approximately 75 percent. In the first part of the century a representative sample of business corporations tended to hold quick liquidity close to the 70 percent level; by 1980 they were down to about 16 percent. Finally, even prior to the worst panics in twentieth-century history, the banks and the thrift institutions always maintained depositor's equity above 20 percent (a deposit-loan ratio below 80 percent). By 1980 it had plunged to 13 percent!

Previous panics and crashes had been relatively isolated, limited to one geographic area, to one privileged socioeconomic class, to a few powerful cliques, to the weakest sectors of the economy. Previous panics were always cushioned by relatively liquid or flexible groups, who reduced the steepness, the speed, and the depth of the declines—the Morgan group that helped limit the

16. WORST LIQUIDITY OF THE TWENTIETH CENTURY

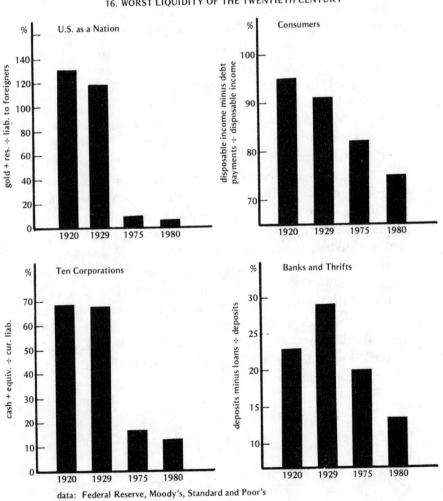

data: Federal Reserve, Moody's, Standard and Poor's

1907 panic largely to New York City; the Du Ponts and powerful banking houses that provided the support for General Motors, Goodyear, and others during the 1920-21 crash; and, most important, the giant manufacturers and the Federal Government, which used the hoards of cash and gold reserves accumulated during the roaring twenties to pull the nation out of the Depression, win the Second World War, and form the military-industrial complex. But after the Great Money Panic no single source of support dominated the scene. The giant corporations and other powerful economic groups finally convinced the Administration to loan funds directly to bankrupt corporations, but this plan immediately backfired and was soon abandoned as an unrealistic alternative. The Great Money Panic was a free fall, virtually straight down, except for psychological lifts and several stock-market rallies.

Previously, the stock market had been the centerpiece of the crash. In the Great Money Panic the stock market was rather the symbol of a far broader and more pervasive panic directly affecting all markets—financial, wholesale, retail, and international. In short, the ghosts and witches of all past crises converged into one time-space coordinate for a reunion with history and posterity. And that's where most of the similarities ended: Unlike previous panics, there were also less tangible, but no less powerful, positive factors—modern communications, sophistication in nonviolent conflict resolution, and international cooperation. Fortunately, unlike previous generations, most Americans had the cool to withstand the psychological pressures brought on by the sudden occurrence of inexplicable events. They had been bombarded by many shocking episodes in recent decades and had been "future shocked" to a higher level of tolerance for rapid change. Unfortunately, there were also many exceptions.

16

The Core
of the Panic

AS THE TOP-HEAVY American economy teetered momentarily
on the tightrope between rapid acceleration and rapid deceleration,
and with the Government still frozen in limbo, the Great Money
Panic began. It did not begin on the floor of the New York Stock
Exchange. It did not begin in London or Tokyo. The panic began in
the New York debt markets—in the nooks and crannies of Wall
Street, behind the closed doors of the phone-cluttered, smoke-filled
trading rooms of banks and brokerage houses.

The debt markets were the core of the Great Money Panic, the
nucleus, the powerhouse that transmitted the shock waves of panic
to the four corners of the so-called civilized world.

The debt markets? Who ever knew or cared to know about the
debt markets? The American public didn't know. The Wall
Streeters, people who lived by the ticker tapes and read the *Wall
Street Journal* religiously, didn't know. The stockbrokers, who
watched interest rates carefully, often didn't know. Virtually every-

one confessed his ignorance of the "highly sophisticated debt-market transactions." Thus it came as quite a shock when the bond-market debacle of October 1979 turned out to be the historical equivalent of the stock-market crash of October 1929.

One of the difficulties in understanding the debt markets was that they were so amorphous, so ill-defined, so scattered, so difficult to see, let alone control or regulate. The debt markets were managed by small groups of specialists linked through direct telephone lines and teletypes to banks and brokerage houses all over the country. They operated out of "money-market trading rooms," appendages attached to firms of all kinds: Salomon Brothers, Goldman Sachs, Merrill Lynch, First Boston, Eastman Dillon, Bache, Morgan Guaranty, Chase Manhattan, Chemical Bank, Manufacturers Hanover Trust, Bank of America, Citicorp, and many others.

The debt markets included the government bond market, the corporate bond market, the municipal bond market, and the foreign bond market, the commercial paper market, the federal funds market, and the bankers acceptance market. It was in the debt markets that corporations, banks, countries, states, cities, and Uncle Sam himself borrowed the money needed to feed their insatiable appetite for fresh cash.

On a normal day federal funds traded up to $25 to $30 billion; Treasury bills and other Government securities, between $35 and $40 billion; and other bond markets and commercial paper, an additional $10 billion or so. But the early days of the Great Money Panic were far from normal. The market went dead and volume slowed to a trickle, while the Treasury held its regular auction of bills. For several weeks the traders were disturbed by the unsettling silence. Commercial banks were attempting to hold the prime rate around 15 percent, but market interest rates edged up steadily. Washington was paralyzed, and no dramatic economic actions were taken to break the spell. It seemed as if the earth had frozen in its orbit. The phones buzzed less frequently, and the traders spoke less loudly across the tables.

Then disaster struck. Rumors of the collapse of a retail giant came over the wires and burst into the trading rooms like a spark in a tank of natural gas. As if by some prearranged signal, all the phones began buzzing at once.

At Garvin Bantel—federal funds specialists—a middle-aged woman with several trading assistants buys and sells federal funds at the dizzying pace of many millions of dollars a minute. Juggling two phone receivers at a time, she rattles off to her assistants, alternating from one to the other: "Get ten million for First Mary—five million for Great Neck—twenty million for Security First. Try First National of Palm Beach—Florida National— Suburban in Washington, and some of our best sources in Chicago and the Coast. This is a madhouse. They need it fast!" But soon, while one assistant is on the wire trying to get cash reserves from First Chicago, First Chicago is talking to his colleague on the other line trying to get cash reserves for itself; Garvin Bantel fed-fund traders find that the banks that would normally be good sources are now asking for money for themselves. Meantime the list of pending requests for federal funds has mushroomed.

"There's only one way to place this stuff, there's only one way to fill these orders. Bid up to 16 percent, 18 percent. No, make it 20 percent if you have to."

"What? This is crazy, an 8 percent hike in half an hour? This isn't even bank-settlement day, this is a wild, wild market!"

A few blocks away at Goldman Sachs—specialists in commercial paper—offers are pouring in to sell the IOUs of retailing firms. It's an avalanche. "Reserve Fund wants us to take twenty million, Atlantic is offering ten million," yells one trader.

"Morgan wants to get rid of a whole raft of the stuff. Looks like they want us to take their whole stockpile," shouts another.

"And listen to this," cuts in a third. "I hear ABC Financial wants us to place new paper for them, and they'll give us carte blanche on rates up to 120 days—fifty million in all! Haven't they heard the rumors?"

Also hit hard are Government security traders at Merrill Lynch, Salomon Brothers, and First Boston. Traders wince as big institutional customers shout over the phone demanding immediate action on the sale of big blocks of Treasury bills, notes, and long-term bonds. But the traders all but ignore them. Their first concern is to liquidate, as soon as possible, their own inventories of government securities accumulated over the past few weeks in anticipation of *higher* prices.

"What's wrong with these guys? Don't they know there's a recession going on out there? Don't they know that interest rates always go *down* in a recession? Listen to this idiot? He doesn't want to buy this T-bill unless we give him 125 basic points above the market. The market for the 2/15 bill is 14.05, right?"

"Nope. It's 15.30!"

"What? You gotta be out of your mind! I just checked it a second ago, and it was 14.05!"

"Check again."

"You're right. No, wait a minute. It just hit 15.60, and in a few minutes it'll be at new all-time highs! Can someone please explain to me what's happening?"

During the bond-market collapse of 1979-80, bond experts felt they at least understood "the causes": the Soviet invasion of Afghanistan, talk of a new cold war economy, and fears of hyperinflation. But now, when another even more severe bond-market collapse arrived—this time in the midst of a sinking economy—most analysts were flabbergasted. They thought that, due to the recession, corporations would naturally cut back on investments, reduce their demand for money, allow rates to decline, and help bond prices to go up. But they hadn't counted on the corporations' *emergency* demand for money.

When the rumors began flying that a giant retailer was going to default on its commercial paper, investors recoiled in terror. Had this occurred back in December 1974, it wouldn't have been as bad. In those days there was only $41 billion in commercial paper outstanding, roughly one-third as much as the commercial and industrial loans on the books of weekly reporting banks. But as of May 1980 it was closer to $124 billion, almost equivalent in volume to the commercial and industrial loans; and during the Great Money Panic it was even larger. As a result, when the commercial-paper market closed down, the corporations rushed to the banks, and bank-loan demand practically doubled overnight.

"Look here," said a corporate finance executive to a bank loan officer. "We have a long-lasting relationship with you, nailed down by our revolving credit agreement."

"Yes, but—"

"You promised to provide the loans at the going rate at any time, and we've paid you up to a half a percent a year for that promise."

"But," complained the banker, "we have only $500 million in lendable reserves and $3 billion in revolving credit agreements. We're going to have to raise the prime and—"

"I don't care what the rate is. We need that money. Now!"

The prime rate soared—20 percent, 25 percent. The commercial banks, owning 15 percent of all Treasury securities and 44 percent of all municipal bonds, had no choice but to begin dumping them in a desperate attempt to raise the cash for their equally desperate corporate customers.

This was bad news for the municipal governments. When the banks dumped municipal bonds, prices plummeted and yields soared—well beyond the limits prescribed by local laws for *new* municipal bond issues. At the same time, cities were being cut off from federal revenue sharing, and their tax revenues fell sharply. The normal avenue of escape—the bond market—was cut off. When they tried to reduce payrolls, the unions stood in the way. When they sought additional help from the Government, the burgeoning federal budget deficit became the big obstacle. There was, however, one last straw: As of March 31, 1980, state and local governments owned about $11 billion in federal government securities. They sold them, and again government security prices collapsed.

Life insurance companies, the biggest owners of corporate bonds—about 39 percent of the total outstanding—were the next in line to dump their holdings. Reason: They needed the funds to meet heavy demands for policy loans—low-interest loans originally promised as a device to promote sales. In April 1980 new policy loans were going at an annual rate of almost $16 billion, approximately ten times the average recorded in the credit crunch of 1974-75. At first they were able to avoid the pain of selling bonds at a loss by taking the highly unusual step of borrowing in the commercial paper market. Then, after interest rates fell sharply in May and June 1980, policy loans eased back somewhat to a $7½-billion annual rate, and everyone assumed that the worst was over. It wasn't. During the Great Money Panic policy loans soared again. But this time the commercial paper market was nearly closed, and insurance companies could only "drop their corporate bonds into the market like the Rock of Gibraltar into the East River."

Casualty insurance companies, pension funds, foreign central banks, business corporations, savings and loans, money-market funds, brokerage firms, credit unions, and even some U.S. Government agencies, all joined in the mad dash to liquidate their bond portfolios and raise cash.

One "interest-rate guru" made the following statement at a much-heralded press conference: "Deflation equals lower interest rates. Lower interest rates mean higher bond prices. Higher bond prices imply more bond buyers. Therefore, current declines in certain bonds are primarily the product of (a) the irrational fears of investors regarding the ultimate ability of a minority of corporations to meet their long-term obligations outstanding, (b) the temporary shortages of cash created by these fears, and (c) the figment of the imagination of small groups of pessimists who dare to challenge axiomatic propositons of the economic sciences."

The statement did not hit the national and international news wires until one hour after the official bond-market close. But the market response came sooner than expected. Thirty-year U.S. Government bonds began to tumble in moonlight trading with big foreign institutions in Tokyo, London, and Frankfurt. By 11 A.M. next morning they were off four points. As Wall Streeters milled around in the noonday lunch crowds, tax-exempt bonds were off five points; triple-A utility bonds were off four points; and some low-quality corporate bonds were on their way to a drop of as much as eight points—the sharpest single-day declines in history. Thirty-year U.S. Government bond yields soared to 15 percent, the three-month Treasury bill rate hit 20 percent, and federal funds momentarily touched 30 percent.

It mattered little that the yield on long-term bonds was well above the "perceived core inflation rate." What mattered was that a trillion dollars in short-term debts were coming due, income was declining sharply, and the sale of bonds was the most convenient way of raising the cash. Obviously, no one was paying much attention to the theories of the interest-rate expert. The big news was the default of major northern cities and the failure of the Administration to take aggressive action on behalf of certain blue-chip corporations on the brink of bankruptcy.

17

The First
Bankruptcies

THE RUMORS WERE TRUE. One of the nation's major retail companies was on the verge of bankruptcy and its financial subsidiary on the brink of default. Its name: ABC Retailers of America. Financial newspapers throughout the country told about the failure of the "octopus strategy," which was designed to raise cash with a diversified range of financial media, but wound up with a dangerous concentration in short-term commercial paper. They told about the fiasco of the "hot potato plan," in which cash that was to be loaned to the consumers for the purchase of durables and other inflation hedges wound up instead in revolving credit accounts. The press did not mention, however, another factor: ABC's banks were dumping their long-term debentures to raise cash for other customers.

One day, when two bank officers compared notes over drinks, they made some interesting discoveries. "We finally scratched up some money to participate in the rescue of ABC Retailers. I don't think they'll get as much as they wanted, but at least it'll tide them over until this great fog overhanging the bond market clears up and they can float that big $500-million issue they postponed last month."

"ABC, did you say?"

"Sure, what's wrong with them? They've got a pretty good rating."

"Oh, no! I don't believe this. You mean you just made a loan to ABC so that they can take more time with their new bond issue?"

"Sure! Why not? Do you have something personal against this company?"

"No, that's not it. Only that this morning I did some liquidating of my own and cleaned out 25 percent of our portfolio, including, believe it or not, $20 million in long-term bonds and $30 million in ninety-day commercial paper issued by ABC."

The money panic was spreading.

Near the end of the boom four big retailers—Sears, Roebuck, J.C. Penney, Federated Department Stores, and Woolworth—were among the most illiquid of the large corporations in the nation. If net inflows suddenly faded, cash resources would be wiped out in a matter of days.

In the 1970 money squeeze it was Chrysler that had gone through this kind of a crisis—a surprise to most analysts because they had forgotten to consider the liquidity positions of Chrysler's captive finance affiliate. This time the analysts made the same mistake. They paid little attention to the de facto Chrysler collapse and even less attention to the plight of the captive finance companies of the large retailing firms.

Returning to the fictional ABC, in the first phase of the panic it was already on the brink of bankruptcy. The finance subsidiary had over $3 billion in commercial paper and bank loans outstanding, coming due at the average rate of $50 million a day. Over $2 million per hour! Meanwhile the mother corporation, which had suffered a big blow when the Fed clamped down on credit cards, was now suffering an even bigger slump because of consumer fears of unemployment. The company had been counting on a resurgence of buying because of the recent return to an easy-money policy by the Fed. Momentarily this occurred. But soon it was being flooded with customer *returns* and swamped in a morass of uncollectable revolving credit.

The sequence of events was quite simple: Commercial paper owners—mostly cash-starved corporations themselves—decided not to renew. The standby credit at the banks, which was supposed to back up this commercial paper, could not be implemented. Attempts to borrow money from employees' pension funds were blocked by the unions. Layoffs were ordered, but there were no immediate savings because of the severence-pay provisions in the new labor contracts. ABC's financial vice-president jetted across the Atlantic to raise money in the Eurodollar market, but returned empty-handed. An emergency meeting called between a group of bankers and Congressmen, which was expected to result in a Chrysler-type rescue proposal, resulted instead in one collective and unanimous shoulder-shrugging session. The retailer had no choice. The lawyers were called in. The books were laid out on the table. It was like Nixon's farewell to his Cabinet—a brief discussion followed by an even briefer sob session, after which the lawyers simply snapped their briefcases shut and walked off to the bankruptcy courts.

The commercial paper market went dead. "If ABC could go under," reasoned the commercial paper buyers, "what about GMAC? Sears Acceptance? Citicorp? Chrysler Financial?" Nearly all issuers, whether solvent or insolvent, came under suspicion.

The stock market, which had managed to flout the recession until that time, was suddenly knocked for a loop, a hundred points within four days of trading. All stocks were hit with big selling pressure—the glamours, the energy stocks, the blue chips, the gold stocks. There were no exceptions. One stockbroker put it this way: "High interest rates and high earnings we could stand. And in retrospect the market didn't really fall that badly considering the prime rate was at 20 percent. Then low earnings were also tolerable because of the good news on the interest-rate front. In fact, by looking over the valley of the recession, we almost got the Dow back up to the 1,000 level. But when soaring interest rates and poor earnings reports hit at the same time, it was just too much to handle."

Stockholders were dumping their shares of the bankrupt retailers. The retailers, in turn, were dumping their huge inventories
of food, clothing, appliances, and assorted consumer articles,
prompting the manufacturers to unload inventories of steel, copper, textiles, and other raw materials. As a result, grain and metal
prices tumbled on the commodity exchanges, dragging down with
them the price of nearly all industrial and agricultural commodities. Soon other industries also began unloading inventories of raw
materials and semifinished and finished goods in order to avoid
further losses. Finally, nearly all corporations rushed to gain a
modicum of liquidity for protection against further money-market
shock waves.

In the earlier stages most economists and businessmen had
anticipated an "L"-shaped recession, a leveling off in the economy
following the initial steep decline. The main reason for their
relatively optimistic outlook was the assumption that this kind of
inventory panic could not occur.

"We've learned out lesson from last time around," they had
declared. "Since we've been anticipating the business decline for so
long, we've kept our inventories trimmed to the bone."

Again, momentarily, they were right. But it soon became
obvious that businessmen and economists were making three
cardinal mistakes.

First, they measured inventories in terms of sales and not in
absolute terms. Therefore, although there were actually more raw
materials and merchandise in stock then prior to the last crisis,
they felt safe because, in terms of "days of sales"—the number of
days it would take to clean out all stocks—the inventories were
relatively lower than the last time. The problem was that they
underestimated the extent to which these sales had been *artificially
boosted by speculative hedge-buying on credit and the speed at
which they would sink when that incentive was removed.* The auto
industry in early 1980 was a case in point. The Detroit PR boys had
for months marched to the tune "relax, relax, everything is under
control." It wasn't long before they were scurrying around Washington promoting the cause of import limitations.

Second, businessmen and economists underestimated the fragility of the financial underpinnings that supported the inventories and receivables of America. U.S. manufacturers had 72 cents in current debt for every dollar of inventories and receivables as opposed to 53 cents in 1960. Among billionaire manufacturers the situation was worse. As soon as interest rates rose above a certain threshold, the pressures mounted to reduce inventory levels. And as soon as the short-term money became unavailable, the sole choice left them was to resort to mass dumping at cut-rate prices.

Third, businessmen and economists, almost without exception, ignored what later came to be called "regurgitated inventories." Marketing experts of that era had tended to assume that if a consumer item was taken into the sanctuary of the household, it was absorbed and, in essence, gone forever. They forgot that consumers, in a financial pinch, could readily become net sellers of durables; that these new sellers could find a ready marketplace for their wares; and that this market was one of the most elaborate networks of secondhand dealerships, flea markets, and garage sales in the world.

Because of the upsurge in inventories and the sharp fall of the cash inflow from sales below the cash outflow for meeting debts coming due, a sudden *emergency demand for money* arose. When this demand could not be met, the alternative solution was bankruptcy, or, as most businessmen hoped and prayed, a Government bailout. It was reported that IT&T was in grave financial difficulties. International Harvester, Goodyear Tire & Rubber, Lockheed Aircraft, and Armco Steel were in grave financial difficulties. Dow Chemical, RCA, Pan American, Ford Motor, and Republic Steel were in grave financial difficulties. Sears, J.C. Penney, and Woolworth, Virginia Power & Electric, Detroit Edison, and Southern California Edison were all in grave financial difficulties. The casualty list grew daily.

Nevertheless, the great bulk of investment bankers, businessmen, and economists still hung onto the belief that, if presented with the cold facts and realities of the crisis, the White House, the Congress, and the Federal Reserve would certainly come through and save the day. They believed that the Government *"had the power,"* that "where there was a will there was a way." They also felt that it was their moral responsibility and patriotic duty to send a delegation of influential leaders to meet with the President and his economic advisers and convince them to do *something— anything!* If the Government did not take immediate action to support the financial markets and prop up the economy, to pump it up and restore it, then, they believed, the nation and all of Western civilization would be plunged into "another Great Depression."

18

Can the White House
Save the Day?

THE FINANCIAL AND BUSINESS leaders urgently requested a session with the President and his economic advisers. In response, a previously scheduled session with the Secretary of the Treasury, the Chairman of the Federal Reserve, and an Administration economic adviser was expanded to include the heads of General Motors, Citicorp, AT&T, Sears, Exxon, Commonwealth Edison, IBM, a Wall Street financial economist, and two top labor leaders. The Treasury Secretary, turning first to the business leaders, opened the meeting.

Secretary: Gentlemen, we have come to a crossroads. We're in a recession, maybe more than a recession, and many of you are feeling the pinch. I want you all to understand that we here in the Administration *are well aware of that.* You want the recession ended. We understand that also. But there is one question we must answer today: Is this the proper time to give up the battle against inflation?

(The Secretary paused and turned to face the Wall Street

financial economist for a response. All he got was a blank stare and so he continued.)

I am convinced that this is not the right time, that it would be premature and rash. I am convinced that if we let up on the battle against inflation now we will soon be unable to control it, that we may never get another chance. If the reason you are here today is to ask for an expansionary thrust—which, by the way, would really be an *inflationary* thrust—well, I'm sorry to say, that's a price we can't afford to pay.

(The labor leaders emitted murmurs of protest and shook their heads. An expansionary thrust was precisely what they had come to ask for, and some felt like leaving right then and there. The business leaders were more conciliatory.)

AT&T: We don't want another boom. All we want to do is prevent a big bust.

General Motors: Exactly! We don't expect a shotgun approach to the recession because we know it would trigger a new inflationary stampede. What we need here is a sharp-shooter strategy that brings relief to key depressed areas and industries without impairing the housecleaning processes of the recession.

Adviser: You're talking about automobiles.

GM: Yes, I'm talking about automobiles.

Adviser: And you're talking about trade protection, I presume.

GM: Not particularly. Our real competition isn't so much from abroad anymore. It's right here at home—the used car market! Only a few months back our primary objective was to shift production from the large, low-mileage autos to the fuel-efficient compact and subcompact cars. But today it's a whole new ball game, the most uncanny combination of circumstances I've ever seen—high unemployment *plus* tight money at the same time! In fact, the two problems seem to be actually *feeding on each other.*

President: You'll agree that we've solved the problem of gas shortages?

GM: Yes, but that has brought us new headaches: Now that we've finally begun to bring the subcompacts to market, it doesn't seem to be making much difference. Did you know that you can now buy a six-month-old, new-model, full-sized car for $1,000 less than a brand new subcompact? And do you know how many gallons of gas you can buy with a thousand dollars? You'd probably answer a thousand gallons. Well, in many depressed areas of the country where the price wars are raging, you can get gas for as little as sixty cents a gallon!

President: All the better!

GM: I agree, I agree—for the long term. But *right now* people are shunning the higher-priced compact cars!

Fed Chairman: I don't quite understand what you mean. Our latest figures show there will be a mild recovery by next spring and, in the worst scenario, a W-shaped pattern throughout the first half.

Adviser: I think it will be L-shaped.

AT&T: More likely V-shaped!

GM: Our business has been dropping fast, no matter what the shape. The last thirty days seem like thirty *months,* so your latest figures are way behind. Consumers have again suddenly vanished from the scene as though in some kind of a silent rebellion. I'm telling you, this isn't your run-of-the-mill, inflation-recession crossroads.

Adviser: What is it then?

GM: It's a tunnel straight to hell, that's what it is. We don't have the luxury of time. Either the Congress and the Fed go out there tomorrow and initiate strong action—immediate action—or we're headed for a first-class depression. The handwriting is all over the walls. Here are some of the facts. First, sales. Although the numbers aren't public yet, I can tell you confidentially we've suffered a 62 percent drop in overall sales in the first ten days of this month. Here's why: When credit controls hit, it was bad. When unemployment struck, it was also bad. But now, with tight credit and declining income at the same time, it looks like the finish! They're not even coming into dealer showrooms any more, let alone laying out the big down payments the credit agencies want. Second, General Motors Acceptance Corporation. GMAC is running into severe collection problems. We can't get the old car buyers to pay. In fact, in one day last week we had more *old*-car defaults than new-car sales. Thank goodness it was only a one-day

aberration. Third, and most critical at this juncture, is the commercial paper. GMAC is running into serious renewal problems. Our
problem is cash!

Adviser: So what do you gentlemen have in mind? Expansionary
fiscal policy? Expansionary monetary policy? Rampant protection-
ism?

Labor: Yes! The answer is yes! Three times yes! You think
Detroit is the only one? We have come here today to submit a four-
pronged proposal for the financial reconstruction of this country.
First, I would humbly suggest that each man here review the facts
further so that we can have a broader grasp of the full dimensions
of the problem we're up against. (There were nods from every one
of the men.)

Citicorp: You can't let interest rates go up any further because of
one obvious fact: disintermediation (withdrawals from the banks).
The thrifts are already losing savings hand over fist. The insurance
companies are losing savings hand over fist. We ourselves are
having difficulty renewing our CDs and commercial paper. If you
don't get interest rates *down,* and quickly, it won't be just the
housing and autos—every industry in the country will be trapped.

Chairman: We tried it before, but it didn't work. We can't stop
the momentum of interest rates. Even if we tried, the dollar would
turn down again! You're worried about money flowing from the
banks to the Treasury? We're worried about money leaving the
country altogether.

Sears: What about *our* cash outflows? At least GMAC can
repossess cars if a consumer defaults on his auto loan. But what do
we do when our customers can't pay their Sears charge accounts?
Can we take back Sears jeans, Sears screwdrivers, or Sears gourmet
foods? Obviously not.

Com Ed: Virtually *all* our services are provided on credit. First
the customer consumes the power. *Then,* he pays his bills; at least
he's supposed to pay his bills.

Adviser: You've got the customer's deposit, don't you?

Com Ed: Yes. But if you think delayed or defaulted bill payments
hurt cash flow, just imagine how our cash flow is being affected by
outright service cutoffs!

(The Treasury Secretary had anticipated that acute cash shortages might turn out to be one of the focal points of the discussion.
It was for this reason that he had invited representatives of IBM
and Exxon to the meeting. He had not yet worked out in his own
mind the exact mechanics of his plan, but he felt confident that
with the help of these two cash-rich companies—and others like
them—he might be able to put together a rescue package that
would head off the impending bankruptcy crisis while protecting
the sanctity of private enterprise. When he asked these firms about
their "cash hoard," however, he was visibly shaken by the response.)

IBM: What cash hoard? You must be referring to the situation
back in the mid-seventies. In 1976 we had over $200 million in
bank deposits and almost $6 billion in marketable securities—
$1.51 of cash and equivalent to cover every dollar of short-term
debts. But not today. By the first quarter of 1980 our quick liquidity
had fallen to fifty-five cents, and now we're down below twenty
cents!

Treasury Secretary: I don't understand.

IBM: We had to expand into new products. We were afraid we
were going to miss the boat in the small computer field. We almost
did, too, until, that is, we began pouring solid cash into it. Then
came the big worldwide shift from outright purchases of machines
to the rental of machines, requiring over $4 billion in cash in 1979
alone. Most recently, our earnings have been hit by the most
unexpected problem of all.

Treasury Secretary: What's that?

IBM: The dollar rally! Suppose we sold a computer in West
Germany in the first quarter of 1971 for a million marks. In the
U.S. we chalked up $250,000 in sales. Now, let's say we sold an
equivalent computer in the first quarter of 1980 for the same
price—a million marks. Nothing changed in West Germany. But
because the mark was now worth twice as much compared with the
dollar, the sale was recorded as $500,000, an increase of 100
percent over 1971. As long as the dollar continued to sink, we
could continue to reap these profits; and as long as the dollar failed
to rally sharply, most analysts were still oblivious of the real

source. But now, with the dollar rallying because of higher U.S. interest rates, IBM profits from abroad are suddenly taking a nose dive.

Treasury Secretary: Certainly the *oil companies* are liquid!

Exxon: The oil companies are liquid all right—liquid in oil. We've got 360 days of oil stockpiled. Almost a full year's supply!

Treasury Secretary: Three hundred and sixty days? Are you serious?

Exxon: You bet your life I'm serious. We thought the big oil glut was temporary, that demand for oil products in the U.S. would pick up with the recovery. We were wrong. Demand for gasoline has taken another plunge. At first we hoped the price wars would alleviate some of the supply pressures, but they're having the opposite effect. People are postponing their vacations, saying it will be cheaper to travel next month or next year. So now we've got 360 days of oil, and yes, gentlemen, we're relatively *low on cash*. We've got a quick liquidity of 13 percent, less than half of what we had in December 1979. Probably about the same as General Motors, I presume.

GM: No! At this late date, if nothing is done to stop the panic, we—will—run—out—of—cash—in—a—matter of days. Today's Monday, so by Friday we'll have to get an emergency loan or else—

(There was a long fifteen seconds of silence.)

Fed Chairman: I'm not convinced. Don't you see what we're doing? We're falling into the same old pattern. You gentlemen were here in 1966, and then it was President Johnson who gave in. You were here in 1970, and Nixon did likewise. You came in 1975, and it was the Ford Administration that bailed you out. Except that each visit was always a little gloomier than before and always a bit more convincing. And every time we believed it, and we pumped more and more. More fiscal spending. More easy credit. In the past five years we've helped to create over $2 trillion in net new credit, equivalent to twice the total amount of all common and preferred stocks in America just a couple of years ago. Then, lo and behold, came the inflation—not just creeping inflation, but runaway inflation, and you all said we had to do something to *stop* it. So here we are fighting inflation, just as you insisted, and finally beginning to

"LET'S GO HOME—IT'S NO JOKE—"

"SAY! HOW'S THAT FOR AN UNEXPECTED PUNCHLINE?"

make headway. Not much yet, but enough to give us hopes of licking it. Now you come along and say you *prefer* inflation after all.

You're saying that if we don't lower interest rates, if we don't make emergency money available, you'll go bankrupt. But how much more new credit will we have to create this time? Three trillion? Four trillion? You thought the last round of runaway inflation was painful, ate away at profits, eroded the economy? Well, what do you think would happen if we had *hyper*inflation? What do you think would happen to American society? To world trade?

Citicorp: We all know the answer to that. Hyperinflation would destroy the entire banking system, wipe out the value of all our assets—corporate loans, home mortgages, investments, the works. But let's forget the "what-could-happen-if" arguments for the moment, and sit back to examine the immediate situation at hand. If nothing is done to remedy this situation, we won't have to wait around for some hypothetical hyperinflation down the road. The banks would be wiped out *right here and now.* We've all got GM loans, Ma Bell bonds, IBM stock. If nothing is done to prop up the economy *now,* we will have a banking collapse the likes of which we've never seen!

President: Can't we steer a middle course?

Fed Chairman: But, Mr. President, we *have* been steering a middle course, and this is what puzzles me. These gentlemen see interest rates soaring, and they therefore naturally tend to believe that the Fed has been following a tight-money policy. The fact is we've been letting the money supply grow at a steady pace. We've been sticking to our targets.

Labor: Then why are the interest rates so damn high?

Citicorp: It's the big utilities. It's the big auto manufacturers. They're still trying to use the money markets to make up for lost revenues.

AT&T: I think it's the Treasury Department. They're the ones who have been crowding us out of the bond market.

Labor: What I can't figure out is why the banks are raising the prime rate despite a decline in loan demand?

Fed Chairman: Please, gentlemen, let me finish. The latest figures haven't been released yet, but I can assure you that the Open Market Committee has been more active in supporting the government securities market than in any week since I have been on the board.

Citicorp: Aha! So that's why the money supply jumped again by over $12 billion last week!

President: Please excuse my ignorance, but doesn't that mean we have *already* let down our guard against inflation? To be perfectly sincere, these actions by the Federal Reserve came as quite a shock to me.

Fed Chairman: Well, actually, sir, this was only a very temporary measure. You shouldn't let one week's change in the money aggregates distract you from the long-term picture. It should not be viewed as a policy change. Remember, the money supply contracted sharply last month.

President: OK, but what do we do about GM?

Secretary: I can visualize an extension of the Chrysler Rescue Act of 1980 to include the entire auto industry. I see problems, big problems. But I'm beginning to—

(The Wall Street financial economist, who until this time had brooded silently with increasing unease, broke into the conversation.)

Financial economist: Gentlemen! You're forgetting the real problem, the problem that first brought us here today, the problem that crushes every argument raised so far: the bond markets. You can't rescue GM. You can't prop up the economy. I don't care what strategy you use—double-barrel shotguns or custom-made hypodermic needles! Look at it this way: when the bond market virtually closed down in February and March, the solution to the national emergency was credit controls—a radical, last-ditch effort to break the back of inflationary expectations. Now what have we got? We've got recession *plus* a bond-market collapse at the same time! That's why GM is in trouble. That's why AT&T and Sears are in trouble. So what are you going to do *now?* The Fed can't slap on another round of credit controls, because that would knock the daylights out of retail sales and bring on a bankruptcy panic. The

Fed can't buy still more bonds to artificially support the market, because these purchases would pop up almost immediately in the money-supply figures; and when bond owners see that, they'll dump their holdings still more.

President: I've had just about enough of this damned-if-we-do-damned-if-we-don't talk. Specifically, what do you suggest we do?

Financial economist: Nothing.

President: You mean you don't *know?*

Financial economist: No sir, I know exactly what we should do in this situation: stand pat. Look at the experience of past Administrations! Every aggressive policy *action* has led to an unexpected market *reaction;* and every action-reaction cycle has come with shorter and shorter intervals: Nixon's wage-and-price freeze—runaway inflation and the Arab oil embargo; Ford's budget deficits and easy-money policy—the dollar collapse; Carter's dollar-defense policy—a bond-market collapse; our bond-market rescue package —a bankruptcy crisis.

Now, regardless of the consequences, you have just one choice, and that is keep hands off, not because of some invisible force that will magically cure everything, but because, *at this particular point in time, the no-action choice is the most rational and logical one a real leader can make.*

President: Do you want a do-nothing President?

Financial economist: No. What we need is a neutral Federal Reserve. We have to let the market make the decisions. We have no other choice.

(The President's adviser was furious.)

Adviser: Precisely when we need anti-inflation and antirecession action the most, precisely when we have come to a critical turning point, you say we should step back and watch the show?

Financial economist: Don't you see? This is not your theoretical inflation-deflation dilemma. It's a very practical matter. Let me sum up the choices. Take a tight-money road, and we have the liquidity problem. Take the easy-money approach, and you get the inflation problem.

AT&T: Yes. And if you follow a do-nothing policy, you know what happens? The debts come due. With every tick of the clock, the debts come due. What do you propose to do about that?

Financial economist: I seriously believe, gentlemen, that we have to let it express itself in the marketplace.

Sears: But there's no cash out there.

Adviser: What about the institutions?

Sears: I'm talking about the corporations, the banks, the cities, the states. That's what counts. Most important, the Federal Government. How is the Treasury going to raise the cash to rescue everyone?

Secretary: The Government has to save its own neck first.

Labor: We have a plan.

President: Yes?

Labor: In March 1980 the solution to the bond-market collapse was to put into effect the credit-controls provision from the amended Federal Reserve Act of 1969. That was obviously the wrong approach. Now I suggest we use *the remonetization provisions of the Deregulatory Banking Act of 1980.*

President: Please, go on.

Labor: The Federal Reserve has the authority to buy directly the commercial paper of companies in trouble. The Government *has the power to create cash.* The time has now come to *use* that power. Here's our plan. First, we erect selective trade barriers to ward off any future onslaught from abroad. It has been said today that this isn't the primary concern. But we must think about tomorrow as well. Second, we propose a wage-and-price freeze. Third, the Federal Reserve eliminates, as a temporary emergency measure, bank reserve requirements, freeing up large sums of liquid funds to revive the banking system. Finally, the Fed purchases, for its own account, the debt paper of those firms deemed to have a high national priority but a dangerously low cash position.

Granted there are certain problems associated with this plan. One would be trade wars. We propose a Tariff Limitation Act that would prevent any present or future politicians from erecting counterproductive trade barriers. The other problem would be excessive Government credit to, or ownership of, private corpora-

tions. We propose limiting Government purchases to $1 billion
only. This is our plan.

Financial economist: *You can't do that.* You can't do it because
for every dollar you can loan to GM you have to borrow another
dollar from the public. It just won't work. The money market
won't stand for it.

Labor: Mr. President, do you save millions of Americans, thousands of businesses and hundreds of banks? Or do you protect the
money market? The choice is yours.

The President knew it was a risky venture. The Federal Reserve
chairman and the Treasury secretary harbored even greater fears.
But in the minds of these leaders it was no more risky than the
credit-control measures taken earlier. They debated the pros and
cons. The Wall Street financial economist insisted that the only
reason credit controls hadn't worked was that they were given up
too soon. But the others said it was now time to try the other side
of the coin.

Although they rejected most of the labor proposal, over the
following week intense pressures were brought upon the Federal
Reserve to purchase directly corporate commercial paper bonds
and even stocks. Finally, despite strong misgivings expressed by
the chairman, it was decided to make arrangements for the
purchase of $400 million in GMAC commercial paper. In addition,
Citicorp promised to lower the prime rate. Few could have anticipated the full consequences of their actions on the bond market.

The first reaction, however, came from the stock market.

19

The Administration's
Stock-Market Rally

A WAVE OF EUPHORIA burst out of Wall Street. "Our troubles
are over," said the money managers, "let's buy 'em to kingdom
come." The public watched with growing enthusiasm. They
crowded the brokerage houses and were hypnotized by the ticker
tape churning out new highs day after day. People congratulated
themselves for "sticking it out," for "holding on," for "having what
it takes" and not selling all their stocks. Once again the phones on
the desks of registered representatives rang incessantly as their
customers called for the latest price quotations.

The individual investors did everything they used to do in the
good old days. But one thing they did not do—buy stocks. "Who in
the world would ever want to go through that all over again?" was
the way one small investor put it. The real problem was margin.
Not margin on their GM, Kodak, or IBM shares, but margin on
their Mustangs, Pan Am vacations, Florida condominiums, and
American Express cards. Not margin on their securities, but

margin on the hoards of material possessions they had collateralized to buy stocks.

It followed that the rally was just that and nothing more—a rally, a not-so-impressive bear-market rally conceived by the Government, born and nurtured by the big pensions, trusts, insurance companies, and professional traders. Most of the "smart guys" who earlier had joined the liquidity bandwagon now joined the new bull market. "Home again at last," sighed a money manager of a large pension fund, relieved of "the bond-market headache," and back in common stocks where he "belonged."

But the rally ended as abruptly as it had begun. It went dead in its tracks. One day it was going like a shot, the next day it was frozen. Some say the rally was ruined by the sudden shift of funds out of the government bond markets, sending interest rates up again. Others explained that it was so short-lived because the market's rallying power had been exhausted during previous rallies in the first stages of the recession. Still others simply said it was "heavily overbought."

Regardless of the reason, it wasn't the market's action that upset people so much. Nor was it the fact that short-term interest rates refused to go below previous lows. All that had happened before. What was downright disconcerting was that the Government's promises didn't come through. Only days earlier there had been headlines all over the newspapers: FED CHAIRMAN PROMISES LOW INTEREST RATES; PRESIDENT DECLARES INFLATION LICKED. But these issues were soon to become old hat. To say inflation was licked was beginning to sound like a corny joke, since most prices were falling apart. Some retailers were already complaining that prices had gone down *too* far. In some cases Government officials were still receiving statistics showing that prices were going *up* when, in fact, they were already going down. It was one big mess, labor complaining about too much inflation, corporations complaining about too much deflation.

The lower prime rate was another bad joke. Sure, rates went down temporarily, but what good was it if there was little or no money at the banks to be borrowed? Even a top manufacturer couldn't borrow money, let alone a small businessman or home-

buyer. It was like the old story of the corner butcher who advertised filet mignon for sixty-four cents a pound, but had none for
sale; he merely advertised it to attract customers.

The public outrage against the Government began to gather
momentum. For months there had been a major clamor for a
wage-and-price ceiling, but now groups sprouted up all over the
nation demanding a wage-and-price *floor.* Arguments and debates
raged in Congress, on TV, and in the financial districts, but there
was agreement on one vital point: despite the Administration's
success in giving a psychological lift to the stock market, the
Government had failed to prevent a business decline.

There were two reasons for the Government's failure to revive
the economy. First was the disappearance of consumer confidence.
"So what if GM is going to be rescued?" they reasoned. "Why
didn't the Government save the retailers, the airlines, the railroads, the savings and loans?" In addition, consumers worried that
if the Government could not help the big boys, what hope was left
for the average wage earner? For years American consumers had
harbored negative feelings about excessive debts. But they had
been able to suppress these feelings by rationalizing that big-ticket
debt purchases were their only defense against inflation. Then, in
March and April 1980 the Carter Administration's credit controls
brought these fears back up to the surface. Toward the end of 1979
and early 1980 everyone was blaming the consumers for the latest
outburst of inflation. Most people assumed that the Administration economists would come out of Camp David and kick the
consumer in the rear. As it turned out, they did much worse.
Suddenly debts, credit cards, installment loans were bad and sinful,
while savings and traditional Yankee frugality were back in
fashion. The Administration, realizing it had overdone it, later
tried to get the consumer to start spending again. But it was a one-
way street. To revive the latent fear of debts was easy; to repress
them again was next to impossible.

The average American did not return to the auto showrooms
and the retail stores. Nor did he return to the stock market, to the
thrift institutions, to the retail stores except for the necessities of
life. The Government could pump the money. It could not tell

people what to do with that money once it was in the economy. With consumer confidence falling, money went dead like a blood transfusion without a heartbeat. The volume of business and profits was falling rapidly. Moreover, after paying off old obligations, no money was left for generating new business, new purchases, new orders, new capital spending.

The second reason for the Government's failure to revive the economy can be traced to the bond market.

20

The President
Stops the Money
Printing Presses

NEWS THAT THE FEDERAL RESERVE was planning to buy
General Motors commercial paper—and rumors that it would
follow that up with purchases of longer-term corporate bonds—
triggered one of the sharpest rallies in corporate bond-market
history. One triple-A issue selling at 72 leaped in only a few hours
to 79. Another issue jumped twelve points and settled down to a
net increase of ten points. Utility bonds, municipal bonds, and
even foreign bonds (traded in New York's "Yankee" market)
leapfrogged each other. Within hours, however, trading came to a
standstill. If you called your broker, he gave you an "indication" of
the market price, way up in the stratosphere. But it was a fiction.
There were no sellers, only buyers. This was the first sign of
trouble. The second sign of trouble came in the government bond
market. Prices went up, though not half as much as previously.
Trading was active, if only for the first few hours. Here's what
came out on the news wires at the end of the week:

THE DEEPLY DISCOUNTED MEDIUM-GRADE CORPO-
RATES AND LOW-GRADE CORPORATES HAVE RALLIED
SHARPLY THIS WEEK BUT DEALERS AND TRADERS ARE
WATCHING QUALITY SPREADS CAREFULLY FOR SOME
INDICATION OF THE REAL IMPACT OF THE RECENT FED-
ERAL RESERVE PLAN TO PURCHASE CORPORATE SECUR-
ITIES IN THE HOPE OF BRINGING SOME MUCH NEEDED
SUPPORT TO MARKETS WHICH IN RECENT WEEKS HAD
FLOUNDERED TO NEAR TOTAL COLLAPSE AS A RESULT
OF THE RAPID LOSS OF CONFIDENCE IN THOSE COM-
PANIES IN THE PROCESS OF GOING OUT OF BUSINESS. AS
A RESULT OF THESE UNCERTAINTIES FEARS OF ANOTHER
COLLAPSE IN THE MARKET MECHANISM ARE MOUNTING.

Bond traders who saw this report said later it left them blank.
Most, tired of the constant flow of "jibberish," did not bother to
read it. Three days later the Federal Reserve chairman called the
President on the phone. "It's no good. The benefit of our plan to
the corporate bond market is a drop in the ocean. On the other
hand, to the government bond market it's a potential hydrogen
bomb. The quality spreads are narrowing, and in the wrong
direction. Meanwhile, the volume of transactions has diminished
to practically zero."

The President was not familiar with the meaning of quality
spreads. "What are the causes and what are the consequences of
changes in quality spreads?" he asked.

"I am referring to the difference in yield between the Treasury
paper and the corporate paper. A big corporation has always to pay
more than the U.S. Treasury to borrow money. Usually the
difference is about 75 to a hundred basis points (100 basis points
=1 percent). Then, several weeks ago, when the threat of bankruptcy was first apparent, the yield on corporate bonds went to 16
percent, but the yield on the Government's stayed at about 14
percent. In other words, the spread increased to about 2 percent, or
200 basis points. Confidence in all corporations—no matter how
credit worthy—declined sharply. People sold their corporate bonds,
prices went down, and yields went up.

"Now the opposite is happening. Top-grade corporate bond

yields are back down to 14 percent but government bond yields are down to only 13.8 percent. The spread has narrowed to 20 basis points—a very bad sign." The Federal Reserve chairman felt satisfied that he had put forth a very clear and straightforward explanation.

"Well, isn't that what we had said we wanted—to bring corporate bonds back up toward the level of government bonds?"

The chairman shook his head, trying to hold his voice steady so that his feelings of frustration with the President's lack of knowledge of debt markets would not be picked up over the phone. In the past he had tried several times to explain to the President how yields and prices moving in opposite directions always meant the same thing, but that spreads, although moving in the same direction, could mean a variety of *different* things. How does one make such things simple for a President to understand without sounding condescending? The Federal Reserve chairman certainly didn't know how. He spent the next half hour going over the events in the marketplace until finally, after considerable effort, the President developed in his own mind an image of bond prices that looked something like this: (see page 169)

"I see," the President said. "We wanted to bring the corporate bonds up to the level of the government bonds. What's happening is precisely the opposite. The 'Governments,' as you call them, are falling down to the level of the corporates. In short, we are not lifting them up; they are *dragging us down*. The question is: Why? Don't they believe our promise, our pledge? Why haven't we restored confidence? At the meeting it was said that we can *create* cash, that the new law gives us the authority to funnel this cash wherever we please."

"The answer is we *can* create *cash*. But we cannot create *credit*."

"What's the difference?" the President queried.

"For every dollar that was created in new cash-money, ten dollars were lost from credit-money outstanding (bonds)."

The President was getting impatient. "So what's the point?"

"The point is that the credit-money is *confidence* money. You can create cash; you can't create confidence."

"Oh. But why can't the Federal Reserve just buy *more* bonds?"

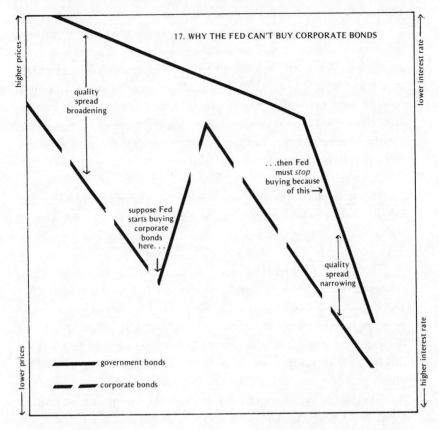

17. WHY THE FED CAN'T BUY CORPORATE BONDS

higher prices / lower prices

lower interest rate / higher interest rate

quality spread broadening

suppose Fed starts buying corporate bonds here. . .

. . .then Fed must *stop* buying because of this →

quality spread narrowing

government bonds

corporate bonds

"When we attempt to support bond prices through direct purchases of U.S. Government securities, the money is deposited in the banks, which means the money supply jumps. This scares bond buyers and causes even greater liquidation of *not only* U.S. Government bonds, but also corporate, municipal, and foreign bonds. If we go ahead and try to make direct purchases of corporate, municipal, and foreign bonds—a radical break with tradition—it will create a tidal wave of selling both in bond markets and in the equally large mortgage markets, financial futures markets, and bank-loan markets. *Nearly all of the $4.4 trillion in debts outstanding are ultimately marketable in one way or another.* Next, even assuming the science-fiction possibility that we could combine the legal authority and the vast resources needed to eat up the $4.4 trillion in credit instruments, it could not prevent the resulting dollar collapse. Finally, assuming we reverted to the sheer folly of permitting a rapid disintegration of the dollar, we would then come face to face with the ultimate wall of resistance. We would not be able to purchase the oil from OPEC countries, who, by this time, would be demanding payment in foreign currencies. We would not be able to provide 220 million Americans with food and shelter, which, by this time, would require immediate payment in cash or perhaps even in strategic raw materials and precious metals."

"But the new law—"

"The new law gives us the *on-paper authority* to buy unlimited quantities of public, private, and foreign bonds. It does not give us the *actual power* to create real economic wealth."

"I see."

"The other problem we are running into is this: The bond-market collapse demonstrated—beyond a shadow of a doubt—that we had reached the point in time whereby stimulative fiscal policies for the purpose of *postponing* a deflationary spiral had become, in themselves, the immediate *trigger* of that spiral. Talk in Congress of tax cuts or more spending raised the spectre of an uncontrollable budget deficit. An uncontrollable budget deficit, in turn, helped to bring about a temporary closedown in the Government bond market. And when the bond market closed down, we were no longer able to borrow the funds needed for the stimulative fiscal policies."

"Congress rescued Chrysler, didn't it?"

"The Chrysler rescue operation, although of temporary benefit to Chrysler itself, did immeasurable damage to the market. It reduced considerably the willingness of banks to embark upon any subsequent rescue operations. It did unquantifiable damage to *confidence*. At first investors thought that the Chrysler bonds were *almost as good as* U.S. Treasury issues inasmuch as they were government-guaranteed. Shortly thereafter, when it was realized that, in the event of a default, there might be as much as a six-month delay in receiving their money, some investors began to get the impression that perhaps it was the other way around, that perhaps U.S. Government bonds were, or might some day become, *almost as bad as* Chrysler paper."

"Why didn't we recognize this when we began the General Motors rescue plan?"

"We did. But we hoped that the marketplace might swallow it. We underestimated the sophistication of investors. They've read all the horror stories about hyperinflation, about social chaos."

"So have I," the President remarked. But he didn't really understand. "You're saying the market is sensitive. I see that now. But—"

The Federal Reserve chairman's irritability was becoming more apparent. "Let's say I own Treasury bonds. This implies that I trust the Government; that I loaned you my money for the purpose of running the Government. Now, you take my money and pass it on to a third party, the corporation. And I say to you: 'Now what did you go and do that for? If I wanted to loan the money to the corporation, I would have done so myself—directly—in the first place. But I didn't. I didn't do it because I don't *trust* the corporation. I trusted *you*. But no more. Now I can't trust *you* anymore either. Now you're just one of them.' So the bond buyer sells the Treasury bonds, and then we are in trouble. Then we, the Government, default."

The President hesitated for a fraction of a second before responding, but that fraction of a second seemed like minutes and hours as the tension built.

"Then what?"

The chairman couldn't believe his ears. The President of the United States had treated the Government's default with levity, utter levity. He could no longer control his boiling frustration— and fear. "Do you want to be the last President of the United States? Do you want to risk a new government with a new constitution? Do you want to destroy, with one sweep—"

The chairman's voice broke with emotion. Silence reigned.

"Mister Chairman, I appreciate the sincerity of your emotions, but you misunderstood me. What I said, in fact, was 'then *what*,' indicating to you my disbelief that this great country of ours could ever reach the point you described so dramatically moments ago. I request you take the following actions: (1) dispose of all GM securities purchased thus far; (2) make a pledge to all those in the marketplace that the Federal Reserve, despite its current legal authority to the contrary, will not purchase, under any circumstances, securities of the corporate sector; and (3) promise to discriminate always between corporates and governments. For my part, I shall proceed to take those actions I deem necessary to correct this extremely dangerous situation."

"But Mr. President, we haven't bought any GM securities yet. We only announced our *intention* of doing so."

21

The
Great Crash

STOCK PRICES COLLAPSED. Corporations and local governments defaulted. Banks temporarily closed their doors. The U.S. Government, however, did *not* collapse.

Things happened so quickly that for years thereafter historians struggled to piece together the actual chain of events. Apparently the Government had been the "very last hope." When the hope was squashed, all efforts were junked, and, in the marketplace, it was every man for himself. Headlines, in which the President, the Federal Reserve chairman, or the Secretary of the Treasury had appeared as the subjects gave way to a new breed of headlines in which the events became the subjects and people the objects: FINANCIAL CRISIS HITS GM AND SEARS. DEFLATION SURPRISES WHITE HOUSE. DEBT CRISIS HITS UTILITIES. One news commentator said that "the only good thing about it is that it couldn't possibly get any worse." Another called it "unavoidable, unpredictable, and unstoppable." Even the President admitted openly that the situation was "bad, very, very bad."

Whenever Administration spokesmen were questioned by the

press about what was being done for the economy, they talked of some new emergency measure designed to plug up the most recent disaster. Then, a few days later, when asked the very same question, "the emergency measure" would be discussed in the same tone and in the same words. Later, reporters were shocked to discover that it was no longer the same emergency. Now it was a new measure, for a new problem, in another industry, and in another region. Fifteen percent of *Fortune*'s top five hundred corporations were clamoring for some form of Government rescue—seventy-five big corporations that had unwieldy amounts of short-term debt that *had already come due*. Now it was the airlines, the utilities, the computers, and even some of the big oil companies.

Congressional committees estimated that, to satisfy all the demands from giant corporations, close to $100 billion in Government-guaranteed loans would be needed. But the most anyone could squeeze out of the banks, including international and Arab-backed consortia, was $10 billion, meaning that only about one out of ten could be saved.

The less developed countries, once believed to be the number one problem facing the world economy, faded into the background. Yes, many defaulted as feared, but the defaults occurring right here in the U.S. were of far greater consequence. "We must first decide," said one liberal senator turned conservative, "if we are embarking upon a life-saving mission or a shipwreck salvage mission. The former would be like a mission impossible, the latter more like a wild-goose treasure hunt. I'm afraid we'll have to let them fend for themselves. Otherwise the nation's credit will evaporate and our chances for a genuine recovery will be hurt." Another senator—a conservative now turning liberal—came up with a proposal for rescuing one "special case" in each industry. Unfortunately, every company claimed that it qualified as a "special case." Still a third senator proposed a five-point standard for selecting priorities, and selected transportation, communications, agriculture, and energy for special treatment. But most companies were highly diversified and claimed that "priority" operations would have to be discontinued unless the *entire* corporation could be saved.

It was of no use; business transactions were decelerating sharply. Bank clearings had fallen 50 percent from peak levels; new private credit virtually disappeared; and GNP was off at an annual rate of 25 percent. Most astonishing of all, for the first time since 1932 the aggregate figures of all private corporations showed a net quarterly loss—approximately $2 to $3 billion per month.

It was the sharpness of the economic decline that gave rise to the "cash hole." Primarily responsible for this phenomenon was the *future commitments* of corporations, which had sent out large orders for parts and supplies that continued to be delivered and, at the same time, were counting on orders from customers that were now being canceled.

Even IBM, one of the most profitable corporations in the world, was within inches of falling into red ink. At the height of the crisis the computer manufacturer receives a call from a giant utility, one of the largest users of computers in the United States. "We can't keep your 3033s unless you give us a 30 percent break on the fees," says the utility vice-president. "We've launched a new cost-cutting drive, and we hope you can cooperate."

"What? Lower the rental price? You know we can't do that. It would wipe out our profits."

"Remember the depression when rents were lowered? Well, now we're depressed, really depressed! So you have two choices. Either you reduce the rental and we keep the machines, or you don't lower the rentals and *you* keep the machines."

"You'd send them *back?* You can't do that."

"I don't think you realize how desperate our situation is. You're worried about losing your profits. We're worried about losing our corporation. So you had better play along with us, or you'll wind up losing one of your best customers."

IBM was forced to give in. But it was only a matter of weeks before the utility launched an even bigger cost-cutting drive and sent back some of the equipment anyhow. To make matters worse, corporations that had bought computers outright now wanted IBM to buy them back. "We have always made it a policy to repurchase all of our equipment that appears on the market and allocate it to new customers," announced an IBM spokesman. "However, in view of the reduced demand and overwhelming excess of supply, we have decided to let the sellers find buyers on the open market."

The money panic had spread to the computer market. IBM sales fell 40 percent. Cash reserves were depleted from over $3 billion to less than $500 million. The company struggled to keep its head above water.

No matter how many corporations were saved by the Government, there were still millions of bankrupt partnerships, families, foundations, and cities. Corporate bankruptcies soared from 0.4 percent to 4 percent; delinquencies on bank loans went from 3 percent to 20 percent; and personal bankruptcies rose from 0.4 percent to 5 percent. One out of every two major cities was having difficulty meeting payrolls. Two out of every three universities began to consider closing down for the semester. It was obvious to most people that the ship of state was manned by a crew of theoretical specialists operating on a trial-and-error basis. There was no broad solution to solve what everyone knew to be a broad problem.

The stock market was hit by forty- and fifty-point declines. One hundred and twenty million shares were traded in one day. In the bond markets expressions such as "fiasco" and "massacre" were no longer strong enough to indicate what was happening. In one dealer's words: "What do you call it when government bonds fall five full points in one day and when corporate bonds fall ten points? When interest rates on a Treasury bill shoot up by three full percentage points? When almost $30 billion in new and old government securities hit the cash market in one trading day? What do you say when a company with a double- or triple-A rating files for bankruptcy and reneges payment on a big bond issue coming due? When events are moving so swiftly that by the time the bond-rating agency gets a chance to reevaluate a company's rating, the company is already insolvent?" For some economists, the answer to all that was very easy: "Values have changed."

22

The
Consumer Panic

A REPORTER studies news briefs and clippings scattered about his desk. They tell of widespread joblessness and the desperate positions of families in debt. He begins banging away at his typewriter:

A new epidemic is sweeping across our country. It's commonly called the "money mania," the "cash craze," or the "dollar dash." The symptoms are by now well identified: an empty feeling in the pit of the stomach, accompanied by an irresistible urge to sell for cash—a growing allergylike aversion to owning material goods of any kind.

Some families are known to dump out their drawers, search their closets, and rummage through attics and basements. They dig up stamp collections, rare coins, silver, china, mink coats, jewelry—anything that can be sold for cash. Many have been seen packing their cars with stereo sets, TVs, vacuum cleaners, and other appliances; driving around town until everything is sold; leaving the car at the dealer's and catching a bus back home. Some of the more desperate families are reported to be selling everything *except* the car. They move out to the country with nothing but a cooler, sleeping bags, clothing, assorted vegetable seeds, and a nest egg of cash hidden under the spare tire or beneath the seats.

Abandoned automobiles clutter the big cities. According to some estimates, as many as 30 million new and used cars are being offered for sale. The commercial banks are in the market to sell some 12 million units, the finance companies, nearly 5 million. Families, private corporations, and local governments are dumping automobiles, competing with the manufacturers for a slice of the car market, or whatever is left of it.

It is difficult to say when and how the consumer panic began. Most observers agreed that it was related, chronologically at least, to the failure of the Government-inspired stock-market rally. Before the rally collapsed, most consumers tried to maintain their habitual lifestyles; investors took a wait-and-see attitude; and corporations at least *tried* to cooperate with the Administration by not cutting production or laying off workers unless absolutely necessary. Before the rally collapsed, there was a thread of confidence, which to some degree held the fabric of the economy together. After the rally collapsed, confidence evaporated. All Government controls, safety mechanisms, and so-called natural cushions were unmasked as mere myths of the past. It was the watershed of the Great Money Panic.

The consumer set into motion a series of unique vicious circles. Imagine yourself sitting in a large auditorium waiting for a seminar to begin. The speaker stares blankly at the audience while an audio technician fiddles with the amplifying equipment. Suddenly, an agonizing shriek pierces the silence. A slight noise, picked up by a microphone and amplified by the speakers, is fed back and forth at the speed of sound and electric current. This was the pattern of events during the consumer panic; every action taken by the American citizen to reestablish his liquidity set off a chain reaction of events beyond his control. These events thrust interest rates sky-high and, in the final analysis, backfired onto the American citizen.

The less the consumer spent, the more businessmen had to borrow, and the more they borrowed, the less the consumer spent. Interest rates moved up. The average taxpayer found that his income was lower. So his tax check was smaller. Result: Uncle Sam, like the corporations, suffered a sharp drop in revenues, rushed to the bond markets to borrow still more money, and sent interest rates even higher. Finally, as savers, Americans were disappointed to discover that there was one textbook theory that did hold up, namely, that when everyone tried to save more at the same time, the gross national product fell, people received less income and wound up with *less* money saved. But that was not all. In order to meet debt payments, they drew from savings at the bank. The bank sold investments at a loss to raise the money. The losses revealed weak capital positions, causing a decline in saver confidence. And, finally, savers pulled more money out, closing the vicious circle. Interest rates soared.

At the big city banks withdrawals hit from two sides. On one side, their own depositors and CD holders wanted their money back. This was to be expected, and the Fed worked with the banks to ease the pain wherever possible. Withdrawals from the other side, however, were totally unexpected. For some time the city banks had been counting on federal funds, coming primarily from country banks, as a reliable source of short-term borrowing. But when the money panic spread to the small towns, the federal funds market collapsed. The small-town depositors withdrew their money from the country banks, causing the country banks to withdraw money from the city banks. The city banks were then forced to cash in more of their investments in tax-exempt bonds, government securities, and corporate securities, and refused to renew corporate and brokerage loans. Corporations and governments, in turn, were compelled to make emergency production cutbacks, resulting in still more withdrawals from the banks.

Remember back in the earlier stages of the panic, when the banks unloaded municipal bonds at a loss to meet loan commitments to their corporate customers? Well, at that time some of the large banks found a temporary solution to the problem: "Wait a minute," said a bank president. "This is ridiculous. Let's see those revolving credit contracts again." They had called in their lawyers, and the lawyers had debated the fine print until finally the decision was reached: renege.

This time, however, there was no quick fix to the problem; they began cleaning out not only their bonds but their loan portfolios as well. "At first," recounted one banker years later, "we decided to call only marginal loans. But we soon realized that our usual criteria for distinguishing the marginal loans from the good loans were no longer valid. Previously, as long as the borrower was making a good profit, the loan was deemed good regardless of cash shortages or big short-term debts. As it turned out, many of the companies with the most promising investment proposals were also the ones with the lowest liquidity ratios. The so-called good loans suddenly turned sour. We could no longer figure out which ones were good and which were bad, and we began calling loans at random." The debt liquidation, previously limited primarily to the marketplace, had now spread to the banks.

The least expected form of credit liquidation came from the household sector. Households were *the largest owners of bonds in America.* They also became the greatest sellers. As of March 31, 1980, they owned $269 billion in government bonds, $75 billion in corporate bonds, $72 billion in municipal bonds and $125 billion in mortgages. When confronted with the choice of selling their durable goods or their investment portfolios, they tended to opt for the latter; and only when that avenue was exhausted did they begin dumping durables in a big way.

One of the factors behind this credit liquidation was the phenomenon called "panic prices," one of the steepest falls in the prices of goods ever recorded. Brand new luxury automobiles could be bought for a little over $2,000. Large color TV sets, which had been selling for as much as $800 per unit, were available for $100. Mountains of vacuum cleaners, refrigerators, furniture, and photographic equipment went on sale for half price or less. Sugar, which only a few months earlier had been in short supply because of recurrent waves of hoarding, now sold for only twenty cents a pound.

Panic prices were being quoted at real estate auctions: $20,000 for a home in an exclusive suburb; $5,000 per acre for land not far from Disney World that, at the peak of the boom, went for $90,000; $20,000 for condominium apartments that previously sold for $60,000; $500,000 for a centrally located shopping center that had been valued at $2 million; $3 million for a Manhattan office building the owner had purchased for $20 million in 1972. Later, panic prices were quoted in factories and assembly plants. An auto plant, owned by one of the big three and said to have been worth over $100 million, was sold for a final panic price of $6,500,000, six and a half cents on the dollar.

Panic prices were quoted at mortgage auctions as the pyramid of over $1.3 trillion in mortgages began to fall apart. Fannie Mae, the Government agency that was supposed to coordinate the auctions, was beset by wave after wave of offerings. "This is ridiculous," said one Fannie Mae official. "In the past we thought it was an avalanche if we got $1 billion in the bimonthly auctions, but recently we've had days in which $5 billion comes to the auction block. Most of it is being offered at a discount price to yield *over 35 percent*, and even then there is no rush to buy." Two weeks later there was a second wave of mortgages of $15 billion. Five weeks later the offerings ran up to $50 billion.

In short, thirty years of accumulation and hoarding were compressed into a few months of panic selling. Fear of inflation gave way to the terror of insolvency. Hopes for material well-being gave way to a struggle for economic survival. There were rapid reversals in values, attitudes, feelings, beliefs, and actions.

23

<hr>

Bouncing
on the Bottom

IN SPITE OF THE TURMOIL, the market system was holding
its own. Because of the bad experiences with the big back-office
paper deluge in the late sixties, the brokerage industry was fully
computerized by the time the Great Money Panic arrived. No
matter what the Dow Jones averages did, and no matter how much
money the brokerage companies were losing, the computers continued to churn out accurate debits and credits, allocating the
supply and demand for securities with efficiency and dispatch. The
computer saved the day for the stock exchanges in Western society.

But in those days few people were paying much attention to the
"system." All eyes were glued to the "Dow." Finally it happened.
The stock market hit rock bottom. Meanwhile, three-month Treasury-bill rates hit 30 percent, and thirty-year U.S. Government
bond yields were at 20 percent.

The trading volume in stocks was unprecedented, but the
averages gyrated wildly, getting nowhere. High selling was absorbed whenever the Dow Jones industrials approached the floor.
It was the beginning of the end of the greatest bear market in

American history. It was not, however, the end of the panic.

Governments all over the world were coming out with announcements to rally their economies. France: "It's time for all citizens of the Republic to reinvest their confidence in their country." Britain: "The real recovery will soon begin." Unfortunately, few people had any savings to "reinvest." There were, however, some individuals and small, unknown institutions that had managed to stay out of stocks, bonds, and other commitments throughout the decline. They had visions of getting in on the ground floor, so they shifted rapidly into stocks and long-term bonds.

In a matter of weeks the Dow rallied back by two hundred

BIG BUDGET
DEFICIT

points; the prices of key stocks nearly doubled; and this new group of bulls leaped for joy. But their timing was off. They failed to consider that there were still plenty of debts, stocks, bonds, and other paper that had to be cleaned out before any long-lasting recovery could emerge. They failed to predict that many institutional investors—banks in particular—still owned relatively large amounts of stock in trust portfolios and would take advantage of rallies to liquidate huge blocks of securities. They failed to anticipate that prices would bounce up and down in the greatest whipsaw of the century before a true recovery could get under way.

Less than a week later there was another rally, this time inspired by a congressional committee that pushed through a bipartisan emergency bill to "reawaken the American public and revitalize the American economy." The new legislation would provide new jobs for minority groups, the aged, and the rural poor, as well as for large sectors of the unemployed middle class. Democrats and Republicans agreed almost unanimously to withdraw troops from overseas so that more money could be "channeled out of the defense budget and into the hands of the consumer." This step, they rationalized, could eventually permit more defense expenses. The program also called for a massive printing of "rent stamps." Again there was support from the conservatives. The program was meant not only for the hard-core poor, but for middle America as well. The theory was that though direct cash payments to the consumer should be avoided at all costs, this "funny money," pumped into the economy through the already established welfare outlets, would encourage the consumer to come back into the marketplace. "It's 'Reconstruction Finance' all over again," commented one top business leader, "except bigger and better. If there is anything that can get these sales moving up, this can." Stocks rallied, and interest rates fell from their peaks. The very next day the question was asked: "Yeah! But where are they gonna get the money?" Stock prices collapsed once again. Apparently, almost any kind of good news set a rally going. The real trick was to get the momentum and *keep* it going. But the big news was no longer coming from Wall Street.

A dark cloud hovered over the Treasury Department. Because of the rising unemployment and declining corporate profits, tax collections had fallen sharply. No one would reveal the precise amount of the budget deficit, but the guesstimates ranged from $100 billion to $125 billion. Finally, the Treasury Department announced a $20 billion package of the deficit-financing issues for sale on the marketplace—$10 billion in Treasury bills and $10 billion in eighteen-month and thirty-six-month notes. The dealers sold the short-term Treasury bills easily because the rates were so high. But the reception for the longer-term notes was extremely bad; the buyers had turned skeptical and weren't convinced that the bond-market troubles were over. Interest rates soared back to their old highs.

Meanwhile, the budget deficit had become a very sensitive issue, and the Administration became more secretive than ever. Newspapers devoted editorials to the "Deficit," with a capital "D": "Will it be $75 billion? $100 billion? The public certainly doesn't know. The President says he doesn't know. Even the Treasury probably doesn't know." Finally the congressional committee released the following statement: "The implementation of the new reconstruction plan will be postponed until there is some improvement in the current outlook for interest rates in the money market."

Despite its euphemistic tone, the statement was received like a bombshell. Reason: the budget deficit was running at an annual rate of $181 billion! Most federal projects were abandoned on the drawing boards; the few troops that did return joined the ranks of the unemployed; and the stock market plummeted back to its recent bottom. It was the last of the false hopes and the false starts.

24

Pressures for a Moratorium

MOST ECONOMIC INSTITUTIONS now came face to face with their day of reckoning. Which ones were solvent, which insolvent? These questions were asked about individuals, retailers, manufacturing corporations, utilities, banks, universities, foundations, cities, states, and even entire nations. The answers had little to do with size or power. Instead, survival depended primarily upon the degree of liquidity reached during the final stages of the boom and upon the swiftness of protective action taken in the early stages of the panic.

The world economy needed a rest, a time for reflection and relief, a cease-fire from the accelerated bombardment of events. The first to feel this need were officials of the U.S. savings and loan industry. A few months earlier, while the stock market was plunging through the lows of previous years, many homeowners could no longer meet their interest and amortization payments on their mortgages. The delinquency rate on home mortgages soared beyond what was later called "the absurdity threshold," the point beyond which written contracts, orders, and promises of all kinds lost their practical meaning.

Who could answer all the complaints? How could they handle all the legal proceedings against those who resisted? What criteria would the s & l's use for choosing the cases to prosecute and the cases to write off as losses? The mortgages, the dispossess notices, and all the other paperwork became just that—a lot of paper and a lot of work. It was an "impossible situation."

A grass-roots movement took hold. Out of closed-door meetings held in the savings and loan headquarters throughout the country came the word "moratorium"—at first only a whisper, but soon one of the most virulent public demands of all time.

Most of the big commercial banks resisted the idea. They still had assets to work with and held firmly to the theory that the banking system, because it provided the lifeblood of the economy, had to be kept alive at all costs. These more powerful banks were supported by the Federal Reserve Board in an effort to squash the movement for a moratorium. A top-secret directive was sent out from the Federal Reserve Board offices in Washington to the heads of member banks across the country:

> Despite the recent demands made by a minority of member banks for a banking holiday, no such action is, or will be, contemplated by the Board. It is the unanimous opinion of the Governors: (1) that the loss of savings and deposits by member banks is merely the result of a loss of confidence on the part of certain sectors of the business community as well as individuals; (2) that this loss of confidence is a temporary development not grounded in any fundamental change in the banking system; (3) that actions or talk of actions such as a banking moratorium, whether partial or total, which could in any way impair the restoration of confidence, should not be tolerated.

While the talk of a moratorium died down, the *thought* of such action did not. Meanwhile in Hartford, Connecticut, the insurance capital of the world, Prudential, Sears, All State, and others wanted a "policy-loan freeze" to prevent the "total disintegration" of their assets; and in New York City savings banks demanded relief from time-deposit withdrawals as the only way to keep their doors open for regular passbook accounts.

Ironically, the strongest demands for a moratorium came not from the savings institutions but from some of the giant corporations. They used the term "production holiday" with the argument that, if only something could be done to stop the drain of cash, business would improve. They also hoped that there might be some way of postponing interest and debt payments without resorting to bankruptcy proceedings and further cluttering the courts. According to one businessman, "The bottom didn't fall out of the market. It was the market that fell out of our bottom! And we're still trying to find it. Our boat is floundering at sea. We ran out of cash-fuel weeks ago, and now we're throwing the furniture into a big furnace called 'interest costs.' But there's still no sign of land." The ship he was referring to was a giant utility company by the name of AT&T.

Many of AT&T's big corporate customers were canceling accounts. Some were going bankrupt. Almost all of them were cutting corners and delaying payments. Meanwhile, smaller accounts, the very same families who were delinquent on home mortgage payments, also defaulted on their phone bills. Revenues, which had been flowing in at a rate of approximately $4 billion a month, slowed down to less than $2 billion. AT&T, along with other utilities, found itself in much the same position as the savings and loans and the insurance companies—with "a run" on its cash resources. Net cash drain ran at the average rate of $1½ billion every month, and AT&T, the largest private corporation in the world, was caught in the same fix as a housewife who could make ends meet only up to the twentieth of the month. The president of AT&T was in a daze. When asked about the moratorium for the banks, he replied: "*We're* the ones who need it. We need a moratorium on our interest payments. We need moratoriums on our debts, on our expenses, our wages, our taxes. We need a complete moratorium!"

Federal Reserve officials and Government economists still remained adamant. They felt it would be defeat without honor. Finally, three developments reaching a climax almost simultaneously forced the Government to yield to the pressures: (1) investment losses at the banks, (2) diplomatic pressures from abroad, and (3) the threat of social disorder within certain cities.

The paper losses suffered by commercial banks in their investment and loan portfolios at the bottom of the February 1980 bond-market decline were small by comparison with the losses at the crux of the panic. As detailed in Table 9 in the Great Money Panic, reporting member banks showed paper losses of an estimated $49 billion in their investments—mostly in tax-exempt municipal bonds and notes—plus losses of $136 billion in their loans. With total losses estimated at $185 billion but only $47 billion in capital,

TABLE 9

Possible Bank Losses in a Money Panic
(of Reporting Member Banks)

Item	Amount Owned 3/26/80	(percent)	Possible Losses (millions of $)
Investments			
U.S. Treasury securities	5,506	15	826
U.S. Notes and Bonds			
Less than one year	7,042	15	1,056
1-5 years	18,049	25	4,512
Over 5 years	4,663	35	1,622
U.S. Govt. Agencies & Corp.	15,764	60	9,458
Tax exempt municipals			
Tax warrants	6,486	20	1,297
Bonds and notes	44,996	60	26,998
All other securities	5,417	60	3,250
A. Total			49,019
Loans			
Federal	21,099	20	4,220
Commercial & Industrial	160,166	30	48,050
Agricultural	4,989	30	1,497
To Individuals for Personal Exp.	73,163	30	21,949
To non-bank financial institutions	46,838	40	18,735
Real Estate	103,256	40	41,302
B. Total			135,753
C. Total possible losses (A+B)			184,772
D. Capital accounts			46,600
E. Possible capital deficit (C-D)			138,172

ta: 3/26/80—Federal Reserve; other columns represent forecasts.

these banks were rumored to have a potential deficit of about $138 billion. Something unusual had to be done to cope with such an unusual situation.

The diplomatic pressures from abroad, meanwhile, were fierce. The American liquidity crisis acted like a cosmic black hole, a bottomless whirlpool that sucked dollars, pounds, francs, marks, guilders, and yen from Western nations as mammoth American corporations and banks made a last-ditch effort to ward off bankruptcy.

Telephone conversations like this between the financial officer of an American-based multinational corporation and his counterpart in London were typical:

"How much money are you holding that can be shifted immediately to New York accounts?"

"Well, I don't have too much in dollars but—"

"I don't care what it's in, would you please give total figures for all deposits?"

"Okay, take it easy. If that's what you want, let me read them off to you—German marks, 254 million, French francs, 105 million, British pounds, 21 million, Swiss francs, 153 million, Dutch guilders, 40 million, Austrian schillings, 26 million."

"Good! Good! Transfer them over as soon as possible."

"Are you kidding? We need the money for operating expenses. Besides, this dollar rally is a fluke. The big play is still to come in European currencies, especially the German mark. My charts, the fundamentals, everything points to a big upswing in the market."

"Cock and bull! That's the same story Tokyo gave me. Except, according to them, the big play is yen, not marks. You want my opinion on foreign currencies? Well, I don't have an opinion on foreign currencies. What I do have is a credit crunch, a money squeeze, a liquidity crisis, and I don't give a damn about the dollar crisis. All I know is that our accounts payable have doubled in the last sixty days, and our creditors are badgering us daily for the money we owe them, and—"

"What makes you think you're the only one?" the man in Europe yells out across the Atlantic.

"If you can't get the stuff over here to cover our exposed rear, we'll all go under, and that includes you, Tokyo, Paris, São Paulo—"

Thus began the mass withdrawal of dollars from overseas. The value of the dollar, which had been wavering from strength to weakness, finally soared. It mattered little what a few speculators thought about gold. What did matter was the hundreds of billions of dollars worth of American skyscrapers, factories, and equipment that demanded the lifeblood of billions in cash dollars to remain functional. The value of the foreign currencies fell sharply.

A procession of foreign central bankers appeared in Washington. They confessed that during the dollar collapse of 1977 and 1978 they had taken the extra windfall of funds that had flowed into their currencies and pumped it into their domestic economies. The West Germans spoke regretfully about major promotion campaigns launched in the late seventies by their banks to attract West German citizens into the whirlwind of buy-now-pay-later consumerism. The Japanese talked about their federal budget deficit, which had ballooned to 14.5 trillion yen by fiscal year 1980, the biggest deficit in proportion to GNP of all leading industrial nations, and how they had been counting on foreign inflows of dollars to finance it. All foreign governments confessed that *they were hooked on the dollar.* "In addition, your money panic is destroying the Eurodollar market," lamented a Swiss central banker. "The trouble is we've built a debt pyramid around it. Our survival, and yours, is linked to its perpetuation. We must put a stop to this onslaught."

It was the threat of turmoil in the cities, however, that finally prompted the Government to act. City employees went on strike. Their slogan was very simple: "No pay, no work." They weren't even bargaining for wage increases. All they wanted was their regular checks. In the midst of city strikes a private communique from one of the Federal Reserve Board members requesting a bank holiday somehow leaked out to the press and was printed in full in the morning newspapers. In certain key areas the banks were deluged with new waves of withdrawals—not just lines, but in some cases mobs of depositors, who overflowed into the streets with angry demonstrations whenever their money wasn't produced immediately. The nation was thought to be on the "brink of disaster." Less than twenty-four hours later, recognizing the economic paralysis, the President of the United States declared a temporary halt to most nonessential production, transportation, distribution, and financial transactions. It was a banking, production, and market holiday.

But all was not lost. There were many who saw the bust coming, took strong, protective steps in the early stages of the panic, and emerged with the bulk of their resources intact. These financial resources, coupled to the still dynamic and solid mass production power of the U.S., would later spark the first stages of the recovery.

BOOK
IV
═══
The
Recovery

25

The Priorities

AMERICA WAS ENGULFED in a spirit of fear. The average citizen imagined that some faceless bureaucrat, in a final act of desperation, might set off not only the money presses but the nuclear warheads as well. The Administration and Congress were concerned that the moratorium would be unregulated and haphazard. Billionaire manufacturing companies feared that other industrial nations would continue to dump automobiles, appliances, steel, chemicals, and textiles, or that their idle plant and equipment would depreciate beyond repair. Wall Street experts worried that stock, commodity, and foreign-exchange markets—if opened prematurely—might exhaust any potential buying power with little movement in prices; and that every individual, corporation, and nation that survived the panic would begin to compete madly for a diminishing pool of liquid resources. Political analysts, on the other hand, predicted that a prolonged economic crisis might bring to power a new breed of quasi dictators backed by military juntas; and that any recovery which might ensue would be sabotaged by civil and racial wars.

All eyes focused on one man: the President of the United States. In the weeks and months following his decision to abandon the GM rescue plan he had grown increasingly frustrated with the advice he was receiving from his closest aides. On several occasions he was said to have banged his fist in an unusual demonstration of anger, saying: "I want a plan! I want a constructive, rational plan!" None was forthcoming.

It wasn't until the final stages of the panic that top Administration officials sought help from a new breed of economists. One of these was George Bennet, "The Little Big Bear." He had recently organized Wall Street's Market Recovery Committee, which would later help to match big block trades for the reopening of financial markets. Another was Mr. Bald, often called "the hermit banker." Following the St. Louis convention, he was chosen to head a new network of liquid banks. He also edited the "Saver Survival Letter," with 300,000 subscribers. The deflation expert was the eldest of the three. In the earlier stages of the panic he had been relatively unknown in the business world, but several months later, when the dominoes began to fall, his name became synonymous with "corporate salvation."

One week before the declaration of the moratorium these "mystery men"—as they were first called by the press—joined with other business leaders for a weekend of intensive talks with the President and his economic advisers at Camp David. The peaceful tranquillity of the Maryland mountain retreat belied the economic confusion in the world at large. But the President made no effort to mask his desperation.

"They're saying they want a moratorium. But what is a moratorium? Gentlemen, I'm afraid it's a dark tunnel, and the only light at the end of the tunnel will be the headlight of a speeding locomotive. Can't we take a different route?"

The deflation expert was the first to respond. "Sir, we are already in the tunnel. We have a de facto banking holiday, a de facto production holiday, a de facto market holiday. We also have agricultural surpluses in rural areas and acute shortages in urban areas. Why? Because we have transportation bottlenecks, communication failures, and excessive cutbacks of essential services in financially troubled municipalities. What we must do now is to consolidate the moratorium, smooth it out, gain control over it."

"What do you suggest we do?" the President queried.

"First, let me cite what we *cannot* do. Many people in debt hope that the moratorium will get them off the hook. This cannot be. We cannot wipe out real contractual relationships between real institutions with a wave of the magic wand. To clean out debts, all of us—businessman, banker, bureaucrat—have to meet face to face and hash it all out. We must reorganize and rebuild, even if it means big slashes, cutbacks, and greater sacrifices—a long, arduous process we won't accomplish overnight.

"Now, here is what we should do: Except for essential goods and services, the first priority should be *not* production, but communication and transportation. While established businesses, schools, and corporate groups are temporarily restricted, the news media plus the web of relationships between friends, relatives, and neighbors should serve as society's second line of defense. Telephone switchboards, TV newsrooms, and printing presses plus land, sea, and air transportation facilities must be kept functioning, regardless of financial difficulties. Congressional debates must be open to the public, regardless of possible inconveniences. The lines of communication between nations must be used to their utmost in order to coordinate an international moratorium, regardless of current trade disputes."

Bennet was the next to speak. "The moratorium can help end the panic in markets. But never forget one thing: Even a disorderly market is a thousand times better than no market at all. You can't close down markets until you have a solid plan for reopening them as soon as possible. I recommend the establishment of market coordinating councils to serve primarily as a communications hub that will help schedule the minimum volume of transactions needed to reopen all markets with orderly trading. The councils gather trading information from all financial sources. They make the data available to bankers, brokers, and investment bankers. Then they match trades—at least $35 to $40 billion in government securities, $3 billion in corporate bonds, $3 billion in municipal bonds, $3 billion in mortgages and real estate, $2 billion in common stocks. They build up support for roughly seven days of average trading. Finally, they reopen markets."

"Easier said than done" was the skeptical response of a Wall Street financial economist. "Where are the buyers? Where is the liquidity?"

The Little Big Bear bent down beside his chair and came up with a stack of computer print-outs he placed on the table. The financial economist glanced anxiously at the names and numbers on the list. Bennet stood up and helped him unfold and spread out the long sheets across the table and onto the floor. One column showed cash resources, one showed short-term debts, a third showed quick liquidity ratios. It was impressive. However, after scanning it for a few minutes, the financial economist was not enthusiastic. "If this list is typical, the task ahead of us will be more difficult than I imagined. Look," he said, stabbing his finger at the green and yellow sheets as he held them up in the air, "when the ratios are good, the quantities are small; and when the quantities are big, the ratios are bad. This is a far cry from the days of J.P Morgan when all the reserves needed to piece things together after a panic could be scribbled on a few pieces of paper."

But Bennet's list was only one of many. For example, Bald said he was ready to move—at a proper time—with large sums of U.S. Treasury bills, Treasury notes, and key foreign currencies; and the deflation expert said he could probably generate a sizable retail demand for long-term government securities while helping to stimulate a flow of savings back into the banks and s & l's.

"Before all resources are committed, however, certain conditions have to be met," they said.

What were these conditions? They talked about the progress of the "housecleaning movement" spreading throughout the country, but they complained about the pace of the progress. Wall Street analysts were saying that the latest round of casualties would be the *last* casualties, that there was no more need for liquidation. They disagreed. They stressed that, by the end of the boom, there had been approximately $4.4 trillion in debts outstanding. *But, at the most, only one-fifth of the debts had been liquidated thus far.* How much had to be cleared out before it was enough? Maybe 30 percent. Maybe even more. They couldn't say for sure. But they were sure about one thing: It was time to halt the chain reaction of panic liquidations and begin a rational, orderly period of reorganization.

One of the Administration officials was visibly upset by the slant of the discussion. Echoing a widespread concern throughout Washington for the free-enterprise system, he raised his voice in protest. "Are you gentlemen implying that the President should assume dictatorial powers under the cloak of a national emergency? Are you saying he should freeze bank accounts, take over private industry, preside over market transactions?"

What he failed to realize was that the Great Money Panic had—for better or for worse—solved that problem. Due to the sharp declines in tax revenues, many Government programs had been reduced to almost empty shells.

The President was particularly conscious of this change. "You heard the man! The Government cannot call a national emergency, because we *already* have a national emergency. The President cannot freeze bank accounts, because bank accounts *already* are frozen. All the Government can do is guarantee law and order, coordinate meetings like this one, and provide the *information* needed to put the pieces back together."

One influential corporate executive complained bitterly about high interest rates. "Do you know how high the prime rate really is?" he asked.

"Thirty-five percent?"

"Guess again. It's really 55 percent! We have a deflation rate of nearly 20 percent. If you add that to the nominal interest rate of 35 percent, you get a *real* prime rate of 55 percent! I say the moratorium will be a failure unless we can get interest rates back down and prices back up."

Everyone seemed to agree. But the President, turning philosophical, made this comment. "This is the first time in history that the cost of money and the cost of things have taken such widely divergent paths. Could it be that the market is trying to tell us something? I'm not an economist. But one thing I have learned is that interest rates represent the market value of money—of credit, faith, and trust. The market is telling us it wants more trust and more faith. At the same time, low prices are telling us that we live in an era of abundance, that we have an almost unlimited ability to produce but have been producing the wrong things.

"The panic is a flash of lightning that is giving us a brief glance into a future of stronger human relationships and more abundant material goods. I only hope we can make a more conscious distinction between the two—between people and things. To force interest rates down will be tantamount to—" The President groped for the appropriate word.

26

A Snapback
in Markets

AT LAST MARKETS REOPENED. There was no big volume.
No fanfare. No sharp price fluctuations. Investors realized that a
real recovery would take time; and the Federal Reserve made it
clear that any attempts to lower interest rates artificially would be
equivalent to "barking at the thunder."

As confidence returned, the action began. Despite the lack of
Government intervention, short-term interest rates underwent the
sharpest decline in history. The three-month Treasury-bill rate
plunged from 30 to 20 percent, and the prime rate was lowered
from 35 to 30 percent. The short-term money markets—the first
to feel the sting of the panic—thus became the first to snap back in
the recovery. The very fact that the banks and markets were
functioning was in itself hailed by the public, and a sudden flush of
funds, hoarded under mattresses or in inflation hedges, returned to
the nation's flow of funds.

The next market to rally significantly was the U.S. Government
bond market—especially medium-term notes. The market committees arranged special swaps wherein investors could cash in

their Treasury bills before maturity in direct exchange for three- to five-year notes selling at deep discounts. This then attracted buying from smaller savers, foreign central banks, and certain highly liquid institutions.

Stock prices, which had begun to fluctuate well above the bottom in the first weeks of trading, finally turned decisively strong. In retrospect, the reasons were obvious: Any trading that was rela- tively free from the panic-and-euphoria syndrome of previous months could attract solid buying from strong investors. In addi- tion, brokers made extensive use of the Government's new Priority Rating System—a computer program that periodically ranked all goods and services produced in America according to the urgency of demand for them. Brokers then coupled these ratings to their own "efficiency evaluations" of a company's productive facilities. Finally, the wide availability of relatively unbiased and accurate information of this kind sped up the process whereby liquid buyers found worthy sellers.

Most of the fears harbored earlier by Americans proved to be unfounded. Rather than an Orwellian world of unbearable Govern- ment interference in the lives of private citizens, the public, using the communications media as their primary tool, carefully scrutin- ized every move of Washington bureaucrats like a big brother in reverse. Rather than rampant trade wars, industrialists throughout the world were pleased to find themselves putting together the foundation for "multinational manufacturing." Slowly at first, but with gathering momentum, mass productive facilities came to life. In the first stages of the recovery, because of depressed prices, foreign exporters discovered that transportation and handling costs exceeded any potential revenues that might be squeezed out of American consumers. Later, American workers were willing to work more hours per year at relatively lower salaries, due pri- marily to a sharp decline in the cost of living. U.S. competitive power was greatly enhanced and the flood of imports effectively blocked.

Most important, despite social unrest in some large metropoli- tan areas, the nation was quiet. Some said it was the calm before the storm. Others explained that the crisis had enhanced feelings of social empathy, and that "the great fear" that prevailed during and after the moratorium was injecting into the behavior of all citizens a high degree of caution and moderation. The main reason, however, was social networks. (For more on this subject see *Social Networks* by J. A. Barnes, published by Addison-Wesley in 1972.) Because Americans had experienced an unusually high degree of geographic mobility, they had also developed an unusually wide range of multifaceted friendship and kinship ties that crisscrossed the nation. This social matrix, although dormant during times of prosperity, sprang into action in time of crisis and became an "emergency net" that cushioned the nation against social chaos. At the same time, a massive buildup of police hardware, plus a high degree of sophistication and restraint in its use, prevented the spread of social disorder.

How long this relative calm would last in the face of continued economic stagnation was a question no one could easily answer. It was, however, with this question in mind that financial and business leaders flocked to Washington.

27

The Potential for Progress

A LONG LIST of witnesses were invited before the Senate Banking Committee to present their ideas.

Witness #1: I am the Secretary of the Sound Dollar Committee. I have come to give you the facts and explain to you why the panic occurred; and to outline some suggestions for stable growth in the future.

Throughout this century economists have overemphasized changes in the *surface dimension* of the economy—the *absolute* measure of strength or size such as gross national product or corporate earnings—while downplaying the importance of the *hidden dimension relative* measures of the system's flexibility and adaptability.

In the graph I have submitted the Dow Jones Industrial average is an approximate barometer of the surface dimension—the economy's overall rise and fall, good times versus bad times. The "equity at the banks" (the inverse of the deposit-loan ratio) is a measure of the hidden dimension—the nation's financial liquidity or flexibility.

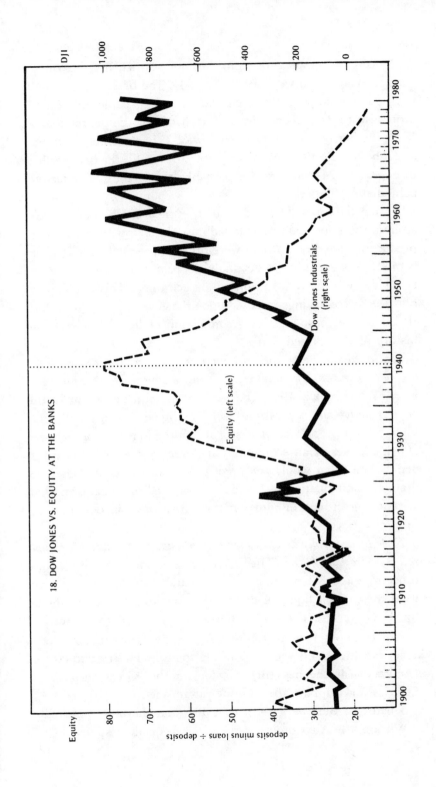

18. DOW JONES VS. EQUITY AT THE BANKS

Equity (left scale)

Dow Jones Industrials
(right scale)

Equity

deposits minus loans ÷ deposits

DJI

Notice how the downturns in the equity anticipated the stock-market collapses between 1900 and 1933. The first drop, from 40 to 27 percent, apparently precipitated the 1901 panic; the second drop, also to 27 percent, clearly foreshadowed the depression of 1914; the fourth decline, to a new low of 22 percent, began at least a year before the 1920 inventory panic; and finally, the fifth decline in equity, to 24 percent, was probably one of the major factors behind the 1929 crash.

During the Great Depression of the thirties, while everyone's attention was focused on the breadlines, the shantytowns, and the production slowdowns, there were other economic forces at work behind the scenes; bad debts and burdensome relationships were being swept aside in a thorough housecleaning. This liquidation, plus the forced savings imposed upon the economy by World War II, led to the most massive accumulation of liquid funds in the history of the United States.

Please cover the graph on the right side of the dotted line, leaving only the left side visible, and examine the graph once more. You're back in 1946. The war is over, but the economy is still not far above the depression level. The liquidity is at an all-time high, but the stock market is still struggling to break through the 200 level. Nearly all economists are predicting a major postwar depression. What would *you* predict? The answer is obvious. The dramatic accumulation of liquidity anticipated the greatest period of economic growth in human history. It showed our potential for progress.

Now please study carefully what happened to the nation's liquid reserves from 1946 on. They were depleted and drained off into concrete and mortar, common stocks and overseas wars. Down went the nation's liquidity, down below the level that precipitated the 1929 crash, and down to the lowest point of the century.

Senator A: Lyndon B. Johnson, more than any other modern American President, was responsible for this. He tried to create simultaneously the heavenly kingdom of the "Great Society" in America and support the hellish war in Vietnam.

Senator B: But the guns overheated, and the butter melted!

Witness #1. All Administrations were equally responsible.

Whenever there was a showdown between an inflation-ridden prosperity and an unemployment-ridden deflation, all the postwar Presidents chose the inflation-ridden prosperity. All were faced with essentially the same alternatives: sacrifice the present for the future or sacrifice the future for the present. And with the possible exception of the last two years of the Eisenhower Administration —at the midpoint of the boom—the choice was "prosperity now" and "the hell with what happens after the next election." Rampant inflation? Destruction of the dollar? "Well," said they, "you can jump off that bridge when you come to it."

Back there during the boom years we could perceive subtle differences in the economic policies of the Presidents. Truman was determined not to become a depression President; Eisenhower was belatedly allergic to inflation; Kennedy and Johnson were out to create a sort of perpetual prosperity; Nixon, Ford, and Carter held things together by letting the dollar fall apart. But looking back and having witnessed how the domestic economy burst open at the seams, having seen the world economy crumble in a rapid-fire succession of unexpected events, we can view the thirty-odd years between the Second World War and the Great Money Panic more clearly; we can see the economic boom in a new light as one long stretch of proinflationary, antideflationary expansionism.

According to the official theory of the day, the economy was functioning below "full capacity," providing the key rationale for added stimulus. The problem was that the theory defined "full capacity" primarily in terms of "full employment"—the level of production that could be achieved if every *able* person in the labor force were employed. The factors whereby a person in the labor force was made "able" or "disable" were forgotten. In short, the official economic dogma boiled down to the tautological, albeit politically handy, statement that "the economy should grow faster because it isn't growing fast enough."

We paid insufficient attention to the structural impact of that unrestrained economic growth upon American institutions, American customs, American values; the individual, the family, the community. We assumed that "nagging social problems" were essentially peripheral to the economic system; that any solution to those problems could come only with still higher growth rates. Higher growth rates, in turn, required by definition more stimulus and more acceleration. To our dismay, despite the larger gross national product and despite massive efforts to funnel surpluses into the "problem areas" of society, the percentage of hard-core unemployed increased, productivity declined, and literacy levels plummeted. Now the decline in GNP we sought to prevent has arrived anyway. It is a dark day indeed.

Senator C: It is not a bit simplistic to assert that the Government's fiscal and monetary excesses were the *sole* cause of social ills?

Witness #1: It would be even more simplistic to believe that the solutions proposed thus far, which amount to nonstop growth in production regardless of content, do not seriously aggravate these ills.

Senator A: Is it not naive to think that material goods in themselves are harmful or perverse?

Witness #1: It is even more naive to believe that human beings can substitute material goods for kinship ties; rely upon social security checks as a mechanism for bringing stability to interpersonal networks; or use electronic media as the sole device for political socialization of youth, for acculturation of minority groups, or for communication between government and people. Human beings periodically need a rest, a time to consolidate, absorb technological changes, and then start afresh.

Years ago our committee tried to hold back the boom and prevent the recent bust. Unfortunately, anyone who was steadfastly against excessive growth and inflation was eventually weeded out of the decision-making process. Today, before we march off onto another boom-bust cycle—one that would no doubt be even more destructive than the one we have just experienced—we must restore the philosophy of *moderation.*

I would suggest you refer to the transcripts of this committee of February 1965, pages 156 and 157, where you will find an appeal by the Sound Dollar Committee for greater control over credit. Fifteen years later, in March 1980, when the month-to-month inflation rate was near 18 percent, the dollar had yet to recover from its great collapse, and long-term bond markets were, according to Wall Street economist Nakagama, "on the verge of extinction," the Carter Administration finally announced a package of "credit controls." Unfortunately, by that time it was too late. The Sound Dollar Committee had visualized credit controls as a *preventive* medicine by self-discipline, not as an emergency cure by Government fiat.

Senator A: What do you propose?

Witness #1: In order to achieve balanced, organic growth, fiscal and monetary policy should be dedicated to the goal of preventing inflation and overexpansion. Rather than merely trying only to outlaw bad times, we should also try to avoid artificially stimulated good times. We must spread material accomplishments over a greater number of generations. Avoiding a concentration of wealth in the time dimension would in itself be the first step toward avoiding the concentration of wealth in the hands of the few—the space dimension.

I make two proposals. First, I propose we gain full control over the expansion of credit. This concept is not new. Preventing the economy from overheating has always been the general intent behind the Federal Reserve's controls over the expansion of the "money supply." It's merely the tools we suggest here that are somewhat different. The money supply has outlived its usefulness as an accurate barometer of economic expansion. For example, the Federal Reserve steadily expanded the money supply from $111 billion in 1948 to $380 billion in 1979. It was relatively unconcerned by the fact that in the same period the equity at the banks declined from 80 to 10 percent, and the short-term liquidity of corporations declined from 68 to 16 percent. Now, because of the forced liquidation of the panic, these liquidity ratios have improved dramatically. We must take this opportunity to maintain each industry and sector of the economy within upper and lower *liquidity limits*.

Second, I propose we encourage a stronger household economy. By permitting households to maximize, whenever possible, self-sufficiency in education, food, and energy—by encouraging the development of intensely capitalized semi-independent production units at the household or neighborhood levels—high-quality, small-scale industry and high-quantity mass production will be able to complement each other. The household can evolve into a reservoir of material, social, and spiritual resources that will protect the individual from unemployment, reduce alienation in mass society, and help the entire country on the road to a more wholesome economy.

Index